contemporary topics in
EXPERIMENTAL PSYCHOLOGY

GENERAL EDITORS: JAMES DEESE
LEO J. POSTMAN

D1263872

HUMAN
CONCEPTUAL
BEHAVIOR

LYLE E. BOURNE, JR.
University of Colorado

ALLYN AND BACON, INC.
BOSTON

Library of Congress Catalog Card Number:
66–19409

Printed in the United States of America

Third printing: December, 1968

Foreword

THE EXPLOSIVE GROWTH OF KNOWLEDGE in psychology makes it increasingly difficult to treat in depth all important topics in a single course. One solution for this difficulty might be called the *survey in depth*. The instructor takes it as his responsibility to cover some comprehensive body of material, but he does so, when practicable, *by example*. The object is to allow the student to work with difficult problems that are representative of a larger body of problems. The survey in depth can accomplish this because any one problem will illustrate the methods, ways of thinking, techniques, and kinds of results characteristic of a wide range of problems. Thus, the study of the perception of brightness can illustrate, by example, a great many of the aspects of the study of perception as a whole.

The present series is designed to present to the student such a survey in depth of the various fields of experimental psychology. The intent of the series is not to provide a comprehensive survey of the textbook variety but to present, as examples, some representative problems within each of the major areas of psychology that are, in whole or in part, experimental in nature. The series is addressed to the undergraduate student in psychology. Each volume could also serve, however, as a basic text in some specialized area, or as supplementary material in a large-scale introductory course.

Experimental psychology is both a series of substantive fields and a collection of methods. In this series, some balance is kept between both aspects

iii

of experimental psychology. Each volume deals with particular methodological issues. The student is not presented with a series of *fait accompli*, but he is introduced to ways in which problems can be solved by appeal to experimental data.

Each book in the series is a self-sufficient unit that does not depend on supplementary instruction or expert guidance. It is this feature which, we hope, will make the books in this series of very broad general interest.

James Deese

Leo J. Postman

Preface

NOT MANY YEARS AGO, there was no experimental psychology of conceptual behavior. While I do not mean to minimize the importance of pioneering efforts of Hull, Smoke, Heidbreder, and others, these were for the most part isolated bits of empiricism and speculation, lacking the coherence of an integrated area of research. In the late 1940's and early 1950's, for some reason—no doubt a complex product of the self-assurance that comes with scientific maturity and the relentless prodding of "soft-headed" colleagues—experimental psychologists began to show serious interest in the conceptual abilities and processes of human beings. This interest has continued to grow and with it has developed an appreciable body of knowledge. This book is my attempt to summarize the contribution of scientific psychology to the study of conceptual behavior.

I owe much to my students; it was at their behest that the work was begun; their persistent questions and insightful criticism counteracted my natural glibness. I am likewise indebted to Professor James Deese; his heroic editorial review and invaluable suggestions reduced my prolixity to often-understandable prose. My wife Vera deserves my deepest appreciation; she not only typed and proofread the manuscript but, most of all, tolerated me during the whole ordeal—all with little or no recompense.

Lyle E. Bourne, Jr.

Contents

Human Conceptual Behavior

I

Introduction to the Area

THE TERM "CONCEPT" has a multitude of meanings. Most of us have used or applied it in a myriad of ways, and among these uses there may not be a great deal of obvious similarity. For example, "concept" is commonly used as a synonym for idea, as when we say, "Now he seems to have the concept," in reference to someone who has finally caught onto a message. Or we may talk of an abstract state of affairs, such as freedom, and call it a concept. On other occasions, a concept seems to be akin to a mental image, as in the case of trying to conceptualize (visualize) an unfamiliar object or event from a verbal description. Undoubtedly, each of these examples captures in part the meaning of "concept." But clearly, it would be difficult (or impossible) to formulate an unambiguous definition from them.

In experimental psychology the term "concept" has come to have a rather specialized meaning, which may not encompass all its various ordinary uses. Psychology is the scientific investigation of the behavior of organisms, which includes as a subarea the study of how organisms (human beings and lower animals) learn and use concepts. In such an undertaking, explicit, communicable definitions of terms are an absolute necessity. "Concept" is no exception.

"CONCEPT" IN EXPERIMENTAL PSYCHOLOGY

As a working definition we may say that a concept exists whenever two or more distinguishable objects or events have been grouped or classified together and set apart from other objects on the basis of some common feature or property characteristic of each. Consider the class of "things" called dogs. Not all dogs are alike. We can easily tell our favorite Basset from the neighbor's Great Dane. Still all dogs have certain features in common, and these serve

1

as the basis for a conceptual grouping. Furthermore, this grouping is so familiar and so well defined that few of us have any difficulty calling a dog (even an unfamiliar dog) by that name when we encounter one. There is then the concept "dog"; similarly, the class of all things called "house" is a concept, and the class of things called "religion."

Each of us carries around a fairly large number of concepts. Most of them we have learned at some earlier time and use in everyday behavior, but we do continue to learn new concepts when the occasion demands. It is probably true that much, if not most, of the interaction between an individual organism and his environment involves dealing with classes or categories of things rather than with unique events or objects. This is fortunate. If an individual were to utilize fully his capacity for distinguishing between things and were to respond to each event as unique, he would shortly be overcome by the complexity and unpredictability of his environment. Categorizing is not only an easy way but also a necessary way of dealing with the tremendous diversity one encounters in everyday life. Concepts code things into a smaller number of categories and thus simplify the environment to some degree.

The bases upon which things may be grouped as a concept are legion. Perhaps the simplest is sheer physical identity or similarity among the instances. For example, we may think of all "red houses" as members of a concept. Here redness and the various observable characteristics of inhabitable dwellings serve as common features. On a different plane common or similar function may provide the basis for grouping. To illustrate, consider the concept "food." There is little physical similarity between a grapefruit and a beefsteak, but the use to which each is put links them together. Other bases (see Chapter II) are even less obvious or more complex. Whatever the underlying principle is, however, it is usually logical, rational, and understandable.

We may note at this point that grouping things together means, in a certain sense, that all members of the group are responded to in the same way. For human beings the nature of this response is often wholly or in part verbal. Thus, most concepts are associated with a general descriptive name or label— as must be obvious for the foregoing examples.

CONCEPTUAL BEHAVIOR

Psychologists are primarily interested in the ways in which organisms acquire and use concepts rather than in any deep philosophical analysis of the nature and meaning of particular concepts. We may dub such activities of an organism as conceptual behavior. What are some of these activities? First of all, concepts just do not come into existence suddenly and spontaneously. Although the bases for a concept may exist in the environment, in the form of things which illustrate it, and although the organism may have the intellectual capacity to "understand" the concept, some learning process has to take place before the concept exists for the organism. Most concepts, if not all, are acquired. Many concepts, such as "roundness," are so simple and familiar that it is sometimes difficult for adults to imagine that learning was ever necessary. But empirical studies clearly demonstrate that even the simplest of groupings are often difficult for the young or naïve organism. The process of learning a new concept is one important form of conceptual behavior and is usually termed "concept formation."

Equally important, and perhaps more common for the adult human being, is a task or problem which requires the use of concepts which are already known. For example, the subject may have to search for, identify, and use in any given situation one from a collection of several alternative, familiar concepts. This aspect of conceptual behavior, which as we shall see has been given somewhat more attention in psychological research, is called here "concept utilization."

SOME HELPFUL DEFINITIONS

The task before us is to outline the current state of knowledge about the psychological aspects of conceptual behavior. To undertake this review in a systematic fashion requires familiarity with basic terms and ideas, so we introduce at this point several of the most common.

Pertaining to the Stimulus

A concept is a category of things. Ordinarily, these so-called things are perceptible and have a real existence in the organism's environment. We refer to them as stimuli or stimulus objects. It is clear from earlier examples that not all stimuli belonging to the same concept are alike. Stimuli vary along *dimensions*, some of which are simple and obvious, like the dimensions of size or color, and some of which are exceedingly complex. An illustrative complex dimension of stimulus patterns, on which there has been some important research, is abstractness (or concreteness). Fortunately, these complex dimensions can often be analyzed into a set of simpler underlying dimensions, but we will consider that problem in a more appropriate place.

Not all of the dimensions on which the stimuli belonging to a certain conceptual class vary are important in defining the concept. Consider the concept "red triangle." What sets it apart from other concepts? Obviously, a particular color, redness, and a particular form, triangularity. Surely neither the size of the stimulus nor any of its contextual features make any difference. In fact, there is a large number of dimensions of variation which are unimportant in delineating the concept "red triangle." In the technical language, we refer to those dimensions which are important as *relevant* and those which are not as *irrelevant*.

A dimension has, by definition, at least two and usually many more discriminably different *values* or *attributes*. For example, red, orange, yellow, and so forth, are clearly different values within the dimension of color (or more properly, hue). Corresponding to the relevant dimension(s), then, we generally use the term "relevant value" or "relevant attribute" to refer to the particular level on a dimension which is involved in specifying a concept. Thus, both redness and triangularity are relevant attributes in the foregoing example.

One final point about the stimulus. Some things illustrate the concept and others do not. To say that there exists a particular definable class of things implies that there are other things which do not belong to the class. Technically, we refer to those stimuli which illustrate or exemplify the concept, for example, a particular red triangle, as *positive instances* (sometimes also as exemplars) of the concept, and those which do not, for example, a green square, as *negative instances* (or as nonexemplars).

Pertaining to the Response

Knowledge of a concept may be indexed in either of two ways. First, to know a concept is to be able to use it. Concepts are used to categorize. Therefore, knowledge of a concept may be evidenced by its use in categorizing a set of stimuli to which it properly applies. In an experiment, then, a subject may be asked to categorize a set of stimuli according to some arbitrary concept (or set of concepts) or to make a *category response* to each of a series of stimuli. If he performs the task accurately we conclude that he knows the concept.

Obviously, the number of different category responses in any experimental problem is always smaller than the number of unique stimulus patterns. Indeed, the number of categories is often two—positive and negative instances of a single concept. These responses are to be associated with stimulus patterns by the subject. However, the process is more than a matter of simple rote memorization of the individual stimulus-response contingencies. The subject assumedly acquires a more general principle which permits the categorization of novel or unfamiliar stimuli as well as those to which he has responded earlier. Commonly, the number of different stimuli used in an experiment is so large that the subject never is exposed twice to exactly the same one.

Second, usually, but not always, we would expect anyone who knows a concept to be able to provide a reasonably explicit description or name for it. Formally, such a description ought to include all the attributes which are relevant to setting apart those stimuli which are positive instances from those which are negative. Often, the subject in an experiment will be asked to demonstrate his knowledge of a concept by producing a description. Rather than categorizing stimuli as positive and negative instances, he may be required to name the concept which a set of positive (and/or negative) instances illustrates. These tentative guesses by S are called here *hypotheses*.

Informative Feedback

A problem is a problem, obviously, only if there is a goal or a solution to be learned or discovered. In conceptual problems, the solution is a concept or set of concepts—either a new concept to be learned (concept formation) or a familiar one which must be identified and/or put to use in some way (concept utilization). The attainment of solution is ordinarily a guided process. That is, the problem solver receives clues from his environment which, if properly interpreted and used, can keep him on the road toward the correct solution. Conventionally, these clues are referred to as "informative feedback." The environment feeds (gives) back to the performer information about the correctness of one or more of his responses.

So much for technical vocabulary. We proceed next to a description of some frequently used experimental paradigms.

EXPERIMENTAL PARADIGMS

A paradigm is a general plan or method for conducting research. It provides a useful and valid set of operations for "getting at" a particular phenomenon. It is not, however, an inflexible prescription for what an experimenter should do. On the contrary, its operations are typically quite modifiable and adaptable to the requirements of each new experimental problem. Further, it consists of little more than a skeleton, to which the particular manipulations and measurements of variables unique to the experiment may be attached.

Although the methodological differences among studies of conceptual behavior are large in number, there are two basic paradigms which are worth singling out for description here. Most other experimental procedures can be viewed as variations on these; significant departures are best noted where relevant later in the text.

Paradigm I—The Reception Paradigm

Most studies of conceptual behavior have employed one or another variation of what has been called the *reception paradigm*. We can trace the use of this technique to the first experiments in the area performed by Clark L. Hull in 1920. The following description of the reception paradigm is stated in general terms and does not represent the exact procedure used by Hull or in any other single investigation.

The experiment begins with a set of general instructions to the subject about the nature of his task. The degree of detail in instructions depends on the particular purpose of the experiment. However, the subject is typically told that his task involves learning how to categorize a group of stimulus patterns. Further, the manner in which patterns will be shown and the kind of response that must be made are outlined. Often, but not always, the stimulus dimensions are described for the subject so that he knows from the beginning what range of variation must be dealt with in the problem.

For simplicity, we shall assume that the patterns are to be divided into two categories and that the subject makes one of only two possible responses to each; for example, either he calls it a positive or a negative instance of the concept. Not all experimental tasks are quite this simple and well structured. Sometimes the subject is required to learn several concepts concurrently; that is, he may be asked to sort the patterns into 4, 6, 12, or any number of different categories, each representing a different concept. Further, the subject may be required to learn unique labels or names, such as DAX or VEC, for each of these categories. Obviously, this complicates the basic problem, not only for the subject but also for purposes of exposition here. Later, we shall discuss these complications more fully.

Geometric designs are commonly used as stimulus materials in laboratory studies of conceptual behavior. The simplicity, familiarity, and highly dimensionalized nature of these stimuli makes them ideal for many purposes. A set of such materials is shown in Figure 1. This population embodies three dimensions of variation; namely, Color, Form, and Size. Each dimension has three values: for Color—red, green, and blue; for Form—square, triangle, and circle; and for Size—large, medium, and small. The population contains designs showing all combinations of values on these dimensions and thus consists of a total of 27 distinctly different patterns. Many different concepts can be illustrated with this population, one of which will be selected for the subject to learn or identify. Take, for example, the concept "red square." All stimulus patterns which embody both the redness and the squareness attribute, of which there are exactly three, are positive instances, and all which do not—24 in number—are negative instances.

The problem begins with the presentation to the subject of some randomly (or arbitrarily) chosen stimulus. The subject is required to respond to the stimulus by placing it in one of the two available categories. Informative feedback is then provided to indicate whether the response was or was not correct. After this the stimulus is removed, and a new one is presented for the subject's inspection and response. The three critical events—stimulus, response, and informative feedback—constitute one trial on the problem. These trials continue until the subject is able to demonstrate that he knows what the correct concept, or grouping of stimuli, is.

There are several points to be noted with respect to this paradigm. First, the stimuli are usually presented one at a time, or by the *successive presentation method*. Because no single trial ever provides enough information to solve a problem, the subject must keep track (in memory) of the events over a series of trials. Less frequently experimenters have used a *simultaneous presentation*

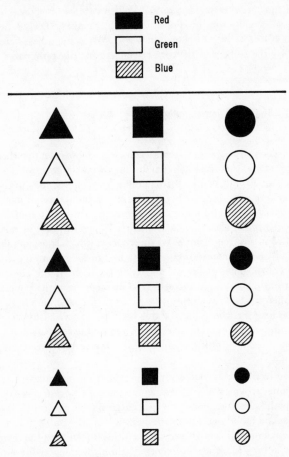

Red
Green
Blue

Figure 1. A set of geometric designs illustrating the type and dimensionality of stimulus materials commonly used in experimental work. The size of this population can be extended either by increasing the number of dimensions (here, three) and/or the number of levels on each dimension (here, three).

method which permits the subject to see all stimulus patterns at once. This procedure can generally be expected to simplify the subject's task.

Second, the subject usually responds to each pattern by placing it in a category. Some experiments have required the subject to give, in addition, a reason (hypothesis) for the particular category chosen on each trial. For example, the subject may say, "I put the last stimulus (a large red circle) in the positive category because I think the concept is *large red* figure." In still other cases, the experimenter may tell the subject what the correct category for each successive stimulus is, and require only the hypothesis as a response.

The particular criterion of problem solution used in an experiment will depend on the actual response required. When category responses are made, the trial series usually continues until the subject makes a fairly large number (say, 10 to 20) of correct responses in a row. When hypotheses are given, a statement by the subject of the correct concept usually terminates the task.

Paradigm II—The Selection Paradigm

The *selection paradigm* represents a somewhat more recent methodological development than the reception paradigm, owing largely to the work of Bruner, Goodnow, and Austin (1956). Preliminary instructions to the subject are, in most respects, the same as those used in the reception paradigm. In this case, however, the stimulus population is presented in full at the outset. The problem begins when the experimenter designates one member of the population as a positive instance of the concept which must be discovered. On the basis of this information, the subject guesses what the concept is; that is, he states some hypothesis about the solution. If the guess is wrong the subject himself is allowed to select an instance from the population and to ask whether it is positive or negative. Once this question has been answered by the experimenter, the subject states his new or revised hypothesis. This process continues—another instance is selected by the subject and categorized by the experimenter—until the subject states the correct hypothesis; that is, the solution.

Because it allows the subject to select his own instances in a problem, this technique provides an interesting measure of performance which the reception paradigm does not. One can determine from stimulus selections (and corresponding hypotheses) whether or not the subject is using any systematic plan of attack or *strategy* in the problem. In reception experiments the subject is in a sense at the mercy of the experimenter for information about the solution. In a selection experiment the subject gathers information on his own. If he knows how to go about it he can use very efficient strategies and acquire the necessary information in a minimal number of trials.

There are many variations on the selection paradigm which have appeared in different experiments. For example, once the subject knows the stimulus population, he may be required to solve a problem "in his head"; that is, under a condition wherein the stimulus population is absent and selections must be made from memory. Under some circumstances the subject may be required to name the category for each selected stimulus as well as a hypothesis. Here corrective feedback ordinarily would be provided after each category response. Modifications of this sort will, of course, be discussed in the context of appropriate experiments.

THE RELATIONSHIPS AMONG CRITICAL EVENTS
IN A CONCEPTUAL PROBLEM

In all conceptual problems the subject is required to learn or discover some arbitrary scheme for grouping stimuli through an inductive process based on the observation of a set of positive and negative instances. Information about the correct concept is presented in bits and pieces, on a trial-by-trial basis, until the subject can demonstrate that he knows the solution.

Each trial, as has been noted earlier, consists of three critical, objective events; namely, the stimulus, the response, and the informative feedback, occurring in that order. Temporal relationships among these events may be particularly crucial to the problem-solving process. It takes time, no doubt, to assimilate and use the information available on any single trial, and if time is limited performance may suffer. Consider the schematic representation of the critical events of a single trial in the reception paradigm as shown in Figure 2. The over-all length of a trial may be broken down into three major components: (1) Stimulus interval, or the period of time during which the stimulus is available to the subject for inspection. Typically, the subject will be required to make his response within this interval. (2) Delay of informative feedback, or the period of time between the subject's response and the presentation of feedback. Experimental procedures typically minimize this interval

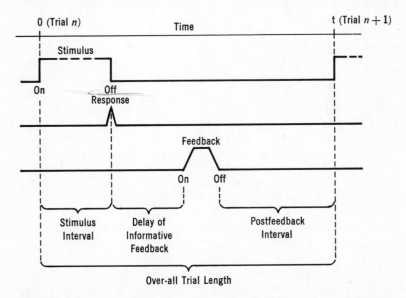

Figure 2. Order and timing of critical events—Stimulus, Response, and Informative Feedback—within a single trial of a conceptual task.

on the assumption that delaying feedback will have adverse consequences for performance, just as delay of reward has often been shown to slow down the acquisition of simple habits. (3) The postfeedback interval, or the time passing between the presentation of feedback and the occurrence of the next stimulus pattern. The length of this interval is particularly critical to solving conceptual problems efficiently, probably because it provides some time to "mull over" all information provided by the preceding critical events of the trial.

The determination of these time intervals varies from experiment to experiment. In many cases the subject is allowed to take as much time as he wishes to inspect each stimulus and/or to make his response (indicated by the dashing in Figure 2). In others the experimenter sets the interval, forcing the subject to respond in some brief period. Those studies (see Chapter IV) which have been designed to explore temporal relationships indicate that their effects on conceptual behavior may be pronounced. They suggest, moreover, that close attention be given to the *control* of these intervals in studies where the major purpose is to explore other variables.

Our purpose in this initial chapter has been to present a small technical vocabulary and a set of general empirical operations that are used in the analysis and specification of conceptual behavior. The availability of these permits us to proceed directly to a more detailed psychological analysis of the problem.

II

Analysis of the Problem

MOST ANALYSES OF CONCEPTUAL BEHAVIOR emphasize the stimulus properties which delimit the class of positive instances. To understand a concept, it is clear that one must recognize all (or most) of the attributes which are important in its definition. Less obvious perhaps is the fact that some sort of *rule* for combining and/or using the relevant attributes is also involved in the definition of any concept. Consider, for example, the concept "red barn." This consists of the class of all things which are both red *and* barn. White barns and red houses do not fit the concept, for both lack one of the two relevant attributes. Members of the concept are denoted by the joint presence of both attributes. Joint presence or *conjunction* is the rule for combining the attributes in defining this concept.

It is fair to ask if the rule for forming concepts is not always the same; namely, conjunction. The answer is no. We need only look at those primitive concepts involving a relevant single feature, such as redness. Here the rule is simple *affirmation* of one specific attribute. But consider something a little more complicated. Let us probe more deeply into the concept "barn." One might say that a barn is a farm structure used for housing cows *and/or* for storing hay and other feed crops. There may be other attributes, but we need only consider two in order to illustrate the point. The existence of either or both of these attributes is sufficient to designate any instance in question as positive with respect to the concept, barn. Formally, the and/or rule is called a *disjunction* of attributes.

The number of different rules that serve to define concepts is large. Many rules depend on the definite presence (or absence) of certain specific attributes. Others are probabilistic, involving only the frequent occurrence of certain characteristics, such as a symptomatic description of a particular category of medical diagnosis. Some concepts are static in that the defining

11

attributes are identified with a single unchanging object. Others might be labeled dynamic or sequential because a temporal order of events, such as in certain weather patterns, defines the concept.

There is no need here to provide an exhaustive listing of the possible rules for forming concepts. More detailed distinctions, such as between probabilistic and deterministic concepts, are more easily discussed later in the context of empirical work. The point is that both rules and attributes are involved in all cases. This is an important point for both experimental and practical purposes; both aspects of a concept may affect individual behavior in or outside the laboratory.

The majority of empirical studies has been concerned with the learning and the use of relevant attributes, commonly in problems where the rule has been spelled out beforehand or at least is simple and familiar to the subject, such as would be the case for conjunctive solutions. In circumstances, however, where the rule is more complicated and/or unfamiliar to the subject, its contribution to the difficulty of the problem may be substantial.

THE DIFFERENT ASPECTS OF CONCEPTUAL BEHAVIOR

If the foregoing structural analysis of concepts is meaningful, psychologically, it should be possible to identify unique behaviors of an organism which are associated with the attribute and rule components of any problem. Such a possibility is implicit in the fact that concepts differ in difficulty depending on whether or not the rule is familiar to the subject. We shall make an attempt next to show specifically how attributes and rules are implicated in conceptual behavior.

The Role of Attributes

Most stimulus dimensions, for example, color or size, are continuously variable. Physical values on such a dimension are, of course, infinite and merge imperceptibly from one to the next. The attributes corresponding to a physical dimension are often best thought of as an arbitrary or conventional category (discrete or noncontinuous) scale, which all or most members of a given culture have learned to superimpose on the dimension and to use for sake of convenience. Each of these attributes is usually labeled with a distinctive name. The number of distinct gradations on this category scale depends on many factors including both the discriminative capacity of the appropriate sensory system and the importance and utility of fine discriminations to the individual (or the culture).

Although we often speak of an attribute as if it were a unitary characteristic of things in most cases it would be more realistic to think of it as a range or category of physical variation. Indeed it is in this sense that attributes such as redness or largeness are primitive concepts from which more complex groupings are derived.

Because the dimension underlying a set of attributes may be continuous there is often a problem fixing the boundaries between one attribute and the next. Where does redness stop and orangeness begin, and how are the requisite discriminations made? As in the case of so many other behavioral phenomena, both inborn and learned factors make a contribution (Hochberg, 1962). No one needs to learn the different feelings that accompany contact with hot and cold objects. Basic aspects of discrimination like this are built into the normal organism. It would be misleading, however, to conclude that experience with the environment is inconsequential. There are at least two learning processes —perceptual learning and labeling—which are important to the discriminations we make among attributes.

PERCEPTUAL LEARNING. Relatively permanent and consistent changes in the way in which a stimulus array is perceived, solely as a result of experience with the array, have been reported. One example of this is the case wherein initially confusable stimulus objects become discriminable with practice. DeRivera (1959) required subjects to associate alphabetical letters (as responses) to different fingerprint patterns. One group of subjects learned a different letter for each pattern. A second group learned only two unique letter responses (each letter being associated with half the patterns) under instructions to look for common features among the patterns with the same letter response. Transfer to a second task, which required associating new responses with each pattern, was significantly poorer for the group which looked for common features, suggesting that these subjects *learned* less about the discriminable aspects of individual stimulus patterns (especially those assigned to the same response).

A related study was performed by Rasmussen and Archer (1961). They gave several kinds of pretraining with a set of unfamiliar nonsense shapes to subjects who eventually were required to categorize the shapes. For some subjects pretraining consisted of learning labels for particular stimulus characteristics while other subjects were asked to inspect and make an aesthetic judgment of the shapes. Those subjects who judged the shapes performed better in the later categorization task. In all probability this result was due to the fact that judgment pretraining led subjects to attend to and to discriminate more effectively among many of the attributes and dimensions of the stimulus shapes.

Experiments like these (Gibson, 1963) point out that it is possible to learn to detect features of an object (or class of objects) which distinguish it from others. There is some evidence of a much weaker sort that the actual sensitivity of a sensory system may be enhanced or that detectable differences between two stimuli varying on the same continuum may be reduced in magnitude through practice (Engen, 1960). Learning to detect previously unnoticed features probably involves learning to use discriminations of which the sensory system is already capable. Changes in sensitivity, however, imply a real difference due to practice in the capacity to detect. Both types of observations have been referred to as "perceptual learning" because they do involve a relatively permanent change in the way an organism perceives stimulation.

LABELING. A second contribution of learning, which is not entirely unrelated to the first, is *labeling*. "Labeling" is a term used to describe the process of associating distinctive names (or responses) with discriminable attributes (or more complex groupings). The fact that we customarily refer to objects of a certain color as "red" implies a prior association between the label "red" and those objects and/or similar ones. There is a fair amount of empirical evidence that these distinctive labels add to the discriminability of stimulus objects and their attributes (Rasmussen and Archer, 1961; Goss and Moylan, 1958).

It is probably true that everyday experience permits the organism to attain many of the discriminations among and labels for attributes or primitive sensory concepts. To some degree the young child's perception of sensory qualities is undifferentiated. For example, twoness, threeness, fourness, and so forth, may all be confused with manyness for the child. Further, the values on the number dimension may be confounded with correlated experiences of largeness, spaciousness, or heaviness. The conceptual system associated uniquely with the number dimension must be to some extent acquired. That much of this process involves learning is best demonstrated by the fact that certain cultures emphasize or impose somewhat different conceptual systems. If, for example, a child were born into a society which paid little attention to the difference between square and rectangle (or parallelogram) his concept of "squareness" may remain relatively undifferentiated even as an adult (Brown and Lenneberg, 1954).

UTILIZATION OF ATTRIBUTES. It appears from the foregoing discussion that learning is involved both in the enhancing of the level of discriminability among stimuli and in the process of labeling attributes. Insofar as the conceptual problem requires finer differentiation among attributes or the acquisition of new labels, (discrimination) learning may be involved. Some conceptual problems, however, are better described as necessitating the utilization of previously learned discriminations and labels, rather than the learning of new ones. For example, when an adult human subject is given the task of discovering the correct sorting of geometric designs into two categories, for example, according to their color, little or no learning may be involved. The task amounts to identifying, on the basis of information provided by the experimenter, which of the already discriminated and labeled attributes are relevant to defining the category of positive instances. In the sense that "new" labels (positive and negative instances) are used in the task, one may think of some associative learning taking place. But ordinarily this requirement constitutes only a small fraction of performance, since it is mediated by already learned labels. The more important requirement is to discover and to identify the relevant attributes among the many that may vary from stimulus to stimulus. To denote this, the task is often called concept identification. More consistent with the terminology used in this discussion would be the phrase "attribute identification," because in the typical problem of this type the rule for classifying stimulus patterns is known to the subject.

The Role of Rules

Conceptual rules are rules for grouping. They specify how the relevant attributes are combined for use in classifying stimuli. For various reasons it is not clear that every concept embodies a rule. But even in the case of primitive concepts, wherein a single attribute provides the basis, there is a rule—either the attribute is present (positive instance) or absent (negative instance)—to implement the sorting of stimuli.

The independence of rules and attributes is worth emphasizing. Some combination of rule and attributes defines every specific concept. "Red and square" is a specific concept; "small and/or tilted" object is a specific concept. Both of these expressions could be used to classify an appropriate stimulus population. But the rules "and" and "and/or" are not bound to the attributes they combine in these cases. Other combinations of the same rules and attributes—for example, "red and/or square" or "small and tilted"—are allowable and meaningful within the same domain. Thus, it is entirely reasonable to think of rules and attributes as independent components of a concept.

RULE LEARNING.   It is probably true that all sorting rules are learned. Through experience with a series of concepts each of which is based on the joint presence of two or more relevant attributes, the individual acquires the conjunctive rule. He learns a set of specific concepts, each of which is based on certain attributes combined by conjunction, but above and beyond this he also learns the conjunctive principle itself.

A simple example of what is involved here is provided by experimental studies of learning sets (Harlow, 1949, 1959). Consider the "oddity" problem. In this task the subject is confronted with a set of (three or more) stimulus objects one of which is different in some specifiable way from the rest. Suppose the stimulus array consists of one square block and two round ones. The subject is allowed to choose one of the objects. If he chooses the "correct" one, in this case the square, he is rewarded with food, candy, or some other incentive. If he chooses incorrectly (one of the circles), all objects are removed and no reward is given. On Trial 2, the same objects are presented in some different positional arrangement. Once again the subject is allowed to choose

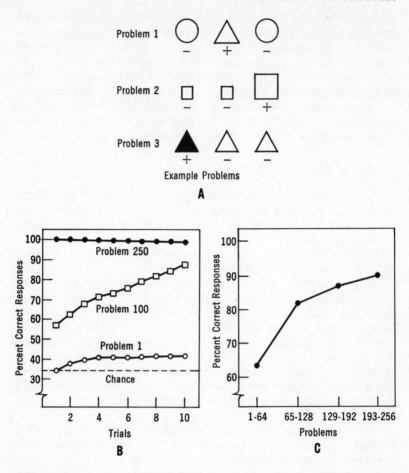

Figure 3. The oddity principle. (A) Three sample oddity problems. The subject is rewarded on each trial only if he chooses or responds to the odd member, marked +, of each stimulus set. (B) Hypothetical data showing performance changes over trials within single oddity problems. The learning function is elevated with successive problems until, after very many problems, performance is errorless. (C) Actual data from a study of oddity learning in monkeys (Moon and Harlow, 1955). The score plotted on the ordinate is the percentage of responses to the odd stimulus on Trial 1 of each problem. After 250 problems these subjects make about 90% correct Trial 1 responses.

one and is rewarded for a correct choice. The problem continues for several trials, over which one can usually expect some observable increase in the probability of a correct choice.

A new problem is begun soon after the last trial on the first. Problem 2 differs only with respect to the stimulus objects involved. Suppose here one block is smaller than the other two. Once again, the odd (that is, small) object is associated with reward. The subject is given several trials with this problem.

The series may continue for tens, even hundreds, of problems. In each successive problem the stimulus objects are different and the particular critical cue or attribute, such as shape, size, color, and so on, changes. But the rule governing reward—associated always with the odd member of the stimulus set—remains the same. Figure 3 shows a schematic representation of several oddity problems, along with sample data.

Two aspects of the outcome of such an experiment are to be noted. First of all, within each problem there is typically a gradual increase in the percentage of correct responses which indicates that at least some subjects learn to respond to a particular stimulus in order to obtain reward. This observation hardly qualifies as rule learning, for the association is specific to a single stimulus. The second, more interesting, facet of the data is the interproblem improvement. In general, performance functions in later problems are higher than the initial ones. Subjects show general improvement from problem to problem—a general positive transfer effect. Subjects become better and better at learning (or solving) oddity problems, and this learning is based on something other than a simple stimulus-response association, for the stimulus attributes change from problem to problem.

Such an observation is probably not surprising to many readers. Improvement over a series of problems of the same type is a rather familiar process. We get better with practice at working crossword puzzles, at writing letters, at memorizing poetry, at solving anagram problems, and so on. Obvious or not, it is an important observation for each of these examples involves, in part, learning rules—ways of behaving which are not bound to particular stimulus features but which can be used in an entire class of tasks.

In the illustrative experiment subjects learned the oddity principle or rule. In later problems subjects chose almost unerringly the odd member of each new stimulus set—the bright object in a group of dull ones, the green in a group of reds, the symmetrical in a group of asymmetrical objects. While stimulus attributes provide the cue, only knowledge of the rule can produce 100% (or any level in excess of chance) correct choices on Trial 1 of each new problem.

The oddity rule is a simple one, perhaps too simple and obvious for most adults to appreciate fully. Actually, it is a simple elaboration of affirmation in the sense that the critical objects are distinguished usually by a single attribute. Yet, the data suggest it is not obvious for the young or naïve subject. It must be learned and it is used without error only after extensive practice.

Demonstrations of rule learning in the adult human being are more difficult to construct. Because of his vast backlog of experience it is almost impossible to find a rule which is completely new to this subject. But interproblem improvement has been shown even for the adult with some grouping rules, such as the disjunction. While an individual may have had some experience with this rule, most people require a certain degree of training to use it perfectly. Ability to form concepts with the disjunction does improve with practice. Data on this point constitute evidence for genuine rule learning in human adults.

RULE UTILIZATION. Grouping operations, once learned, provide the organism with powerful conceptual tools. A repertoire of rules permits rapid acquisition of unfamiliar stimulus classifications based on it, increases the range of concepts that can be formed with any particular stimulus population, and enhances the flexibility of the subject's conceptual behavior, in general. Like other learned rules, such as mathematical formulas, grammar, chess moves, study habits, and so on, conceptual rules implement problem solving, thinking, and other acts of so-called complex or higher-order behavior which are characteristic of the mature, sophisticated organism.

Experimental studies of rule utilization are unfortunately rare. Experiments on problem solving by human adults provide perhaps the best examples of the use of rules. Maier (1930) developed a number of such experimental tasks, one of which is called the "pendulum problem." This task requires the subject to find a way to tie together the ends of two strings suspended from the ceiling of a room. The strings are too far apart to allow the subject simply to carry one end over to the other. To solve the problem, the subject has to attach a weight to the end of one string, set it in pendulum-like motion, take hold of the free string, and then catch the swinging string when its arc carries it close by. The critical element in problem solution is the pendulum principle (or rule). That the principle is not quite so obvious as it may sound is documented by the fact that in Maier's experiment no subject attained solution without some guidance from the experimenter.

A GENERAL SCHEME
FOR DESCRIBING CONCEPTUAL BEHAVIOR

Thus far we have discussed in general terms the various facets of conceptual behavior as it is studied in experimental psychology. Deeper penetration requires a greater concern with the actual theory and research. We pause at this point to provide a brief summary of these facets, to indicate their interrelationships and organization, and to emphasize certain methodological and terminological problems.

Conceptual behavior covers all the activities of an organism which in any way involve concepts. These include forming new and/or using already known concepts in some way. A concept is analyzable into two structural components, rule and attributes. To the subject, whose task it is to learn or discover a concept, either or both components may be unknown.

These considerations produce rather directly a scheme, portrayed in Table 1, for classifying research and theory in the area. The scheme amounts to a simple 2 x 2 representation with problem elements, that is, rules for grouping and attributes, providing the basis for one distinction and the nature of behavior, that is, learning and utilization, providing the other. According to this scheme there are four fundamental types of conceptual tasks or problems; namely, attribute learning, attribute utilization, rule learning, and rule utilization.

Table 1

Schematic representation and examples of tasks involving conceptual behavior

	Type of behavior	
	Learning	Utilization
Attribute	Perceptual learning, labeling	Concept identification, sorting tasks
Problem Element Rule	Formation of learning sets, positive transfer across conceptual problems based on the same rule	Rule identification, problem solving

Examples of each type of task are shown in Table 1. In the attribute-learning cell we include those tasks wherein the perceptual characteristics of a stimulus array are changed, either through enhanced sensitivity to the underlying stimulus dimensions or through learning to detect distinguishing features of stimuli. Under attribute utilization fall those tasks which require the discovery and/or use of already discriminable and labeled attributes, such as concept-identification problems. Rule-learning tasks are those wherein new principles of grouping are acquired; many studies of learning set formation nicely illustrate this category. And finally, rule utilization is meant to encompass those tasks which require the selection and use of known principles, such as many problem-solving situations.

Some Notable Difficulties

A PURE CONCEPTUAL TASK. One may think of the examples of tasks falling into each of the cells of Table 1 as "pure" in the sense that presumably only a single behavioral requirement, dealing either with attributes or rule, is imposed. It is clear, however, that not all experiments or theories in the area of conceptual behavior deal exclusively with "pure" cases. Actually many conceptual problems embody several requirements. For example, some experiments employ a task in which the subject must both identify relevant attributes and learn an unfamiliar rule for grouping. An experimenter need not use pure tasks to gain useful and informative data on conceptual behavior. But it is important to recognize the existing components of any task and to evaluate the results of the experiment accordingly. In this respect the portrayal in Table 1 will assist in the interpretation of later experiments.

THE DISTINCTION BETWEEN LEARNING AND UTILIZATION. Any attempt to draw a firm line between learning and utilization is fraught with difficulties. Suppose we provide some opportunity for a subject to practice a new response or response sequence or to form some new association(s) between stimulus features of his environment and a response. How can we tell when learning is complete, and that the subject is "ready" to use his newly acquired behavior? While it is true that all learning necessarily entails a modification of behavior and that continuing practice tends to yield smaller and smaller behavioral changes, it is not clear that even the simplest of learning processes ever terminates. Furthermore, complete learning is probably no prerequisite to the *utilization* of acquired behavior. Even weakly established associations, for example, may be called into use in a different situation.

The distinction between learning and utilization in Table 1 is then arbitrary. In general, we use the term "learning" for those tasks and experiments wherein the emphasis and central interest lies in the acquisition of differential responses for formerly confusable attributes or of some complex behavior strategy which implements a formerly unfamiliar rule for grouping. When it is clear from strictly formal considerations that learning has taken place and when the task demands some use of that prior learning, we use the term "utilization." It may be noted here that the vast majority of utilization tasks are essentially identification problems; that is, problems wherein the primary requirement is to discover and specify which of several known alternatives (either rules or attributes) is or are relevant to problem solution.

THE DISTINCTION BETWEEN RULES AND ATTRIBUTES. Concept formation and concept utilization entail dealing *both* with attributes and with rules. Indeed, as we have noted, discriminations among attributes and the behavior required to implement a rule are typically acquired within the context of specific conceptual problems. As a result the difference between rule and attributes is not always clear; both are bound up in specific groupings of stimulation which are learned. Certainly, the typical subject does analyze a learned concept into its component parts without external prodding and direction. The properties of rules actually may be thought of in terms of certain relationships among attributes, such as "different from" (oddity) or "joint presence of" (conjunction), and may appear not to carry any information other than in the context of specific concepts.

It can be shown, however, that the rule-attribute distinction is an important one to make. It is possible, in both a formal and a methodological sense, to define a rule, independent of any attributes. Further, it can be shown that the acquisition of knowledge about a rule and of behavior associated with it proceeds separately of attribute learning or utilization. It is on this basis that we draw a strong distinction which we find to have considerable utility in the interpretation of behavior in conceptual problems.

OVERLAP WITH OTHER AREAS OF PSYCHOLOGICAL RESEARCH. Efforts to categorize behaviors are both common and useful. While behavior is basically continuous and multidimensional, for the sake of efficient communication and the organization of knowledge it is handy to have a finite set of categories and category labels at our disposal. Conceptual behavior is such a category.

We should recognize, however, that categories of behavior overlap; they are not mutually exclusive. In part, conceptual behavior involves *perception;* environmental stimulation is received, transformed, and in most cases, organized before we respond to it overtly. Clearly, basic *learning* processes are involved; discriminations are in part acquired, verbal and other labels are acquired, learning sets are acquired. On another dimension conceptual behavior impinges on *thinking* and *problem solving*, for certainly adequate performance in conceptual tasks depends on internally organized symbolic activities and complex behavioral outputs.

Other examples of overlap could be cited. The point, however, is that conceptual behavior as an area of inquiry within psychology is not an isolated body of knowledge. Rather it is a part of an integrated, but incomplete, network of facts and theories which defines the whole of psychology. We shall treat it in this way, calling upon the information available in other categorical areas of psychology which help to make a coherent and intelligible picture of what is known about the conceptual behavior of human organisms.

WORDS AND CONCEPTS

For human beings words and concepts are inextricably bound. It is difficult even to think about any known concept without the immediate intrusion of its verbal associate(s) or description. Not only is it the case that most conceptual groupings have meaningful verbal labels but also some concepts are learned and used almost exclusively in a verbal context. For example, at least some people use and understand concepts such as "electron," "gene," "economic recession," and "nuclear holocaust" without much of any experience with their empirical referents. This state of affairs has led at least one psychologist who has worked extensively in the area to the conclusion that concepts ". . . are meaningful words which label classes of otherwise dissimilar stimuli" (Archer, 1964, p. 238). He goes on to point out the indisputable fact that a shortcoming in ability to use words is the single most important factor in the slow acquisition of concepts by preverbal human subjects and lower organisms.

While the importance of language in conceptual behavior cannot be denied, there is no reason to assume a strict identity of words and concepts. It has long been known that people can learn concepts or stimulus groupings without being able to verbalize or put them into words (Hull, 1920). Still there are at least two fundamental functions of words in conceptual behavior —first as symbols, and second as cues or signs. Both functions are based on an assumption that language is a learned representation or code for events, actions, objects, and relationships in the real world. Words are a cultural convenience which in many behavioral processes "stand for" other things. Clearly, this is a vastly oversimplified description of language, but it is suitable for present purposes.

As symbols, words are internal (or cognitive) mediators of behavior. They are the tools or elements of (most) thought processes. They allow us to think about concepts in the absence of any examples thereof. They are the basis of much covert activity which may or may not be accompanied or followed by overt action.

As cues or signs, words carry information about concepts from speaker to listener. In this sense, words implement communication. Because they are conventionally established representatives of something else which may be awkward or difficult to produce or point out in any situation, they provide an efficient and convenient means for the transfer of information.

Words, then, are responses which have been associated with states of the world. When multiple associations—between a response and several dissimilar stimuli—exist for a subject, the word is a label for a concept and can be used symbolically. Insofar as these associations are the same for two or more people, the word may function as a sign in communication. When verbal labels do not exist, either because the concept is arbitrary and unnatural or because the stimulus attributes do not lend themselves easily to verbal associations, the subject may have difficulty describing the basis for his category responses. This merely shows that words and concepts are independent, though often tied in natural circumstances.

This position toward the relationship between language and thinking in general is similar to that developed by Luria (1957) and Kendler (1961). It stems from a belief that as a child matures his behavior is more and more influenced by self-generated stimuli. His own verbal behavior is the most important source of self-stimulation. Verbal responses, whether overt or implicit, mediate and regulate other overt behaviors. Words as symbols govern much of what we do.

The aforementioned functions are in reality rather primitive in comparison to what human beings actually can accomplish with language. For example, we have said nothing about the syntax and rules of language which specify the meaningful ordering and organization of words into larger linguistic units. But we shall not delve any more deeply into the complexity of language. There is just one further point about the relation of words and concepts that needs to be indicated. Words as signs are external, public, and objective stimulus events. Like any other stimuli, they can be grouped. They serve as the basis for "verbal concepts." They (or their meanings) may be combined, moreover, in new ways, which in some circumstances generate concepts with no known or previously experienced referents. Thus, through words and language the range of conceptual behavior of human beings becomes vastly expanded. So much so that, as Archer implied, it becomes almost impossible in many circumstances to distinguish the concept from its verbal label.

III

Theories of Conceptual Behavior

MOST THEORIES OF CONCEPTUAL BEHAVIOR are special cases of learning theory. This, of course, is hardly unexpected in view of the close relationship between learning and concept formation. When it is further realized that much progress has been made toward an empirical understanding of learning processes, the present state of theoretical affairs rather naturally follows. Commonly, then, conceptual behavior is treated by the theorist as a complicated learning process.

It is impossible to give a formal development and evaluation of each individual theory in this chapter. The scope of the present review is restricted in two ways. First, we consider only two basic themes which underlie many theories and demonstrate the variety of interpretations by describing some examples of each theme. Second, we shall leave the question of the empirical validity of these theories for later chapters. An attempt is made to select the most successful theories for discussion. The task, however, is not simple, for a theory may make excellent predictions in some cases but inadequate ones in others where a different interpretation seems to fit better. For this reason, it is more appropriate to consider how "good" a theory is in the context of specific experimental problems.

TWO TRENDS IN THEORIES

In 1924 Heidbreder correctly anticipated two main lines of development which presently characterize most theories of the formation or utilization of concepts. One line pictures the organism as a passive recipient of information from his environment. Each example of the unknown concept provides him with an additional bit of knowledge. Since most concepts are based on some common property characteristic of examples, which is missing in nonexamples, the organism is able in this way to build up a "composite photograph" of examples wherein the common feature stands out. Relevant attributes (and rule) are repeatedly reinforced while irrelevant features are washed out, leaving the organism with a clear picture of what the concept is.

This type of theory in its simplest form attributes nothing to the organism but a memory for previous examples. Activities or conditions internal to the organism make little or no contribution to concept formation. The subject does not operate on incoming information in any essential way. The subject is viewed as a passive system on which the environment enscribes its information. In its various forms this has been a favorite argument of psychologists who adhere to Behavioristic and Associationistic orientations toward psychology. Concept formation, like simpler forms of learning, is viewed as a process wherein stimuli become gradually connected with some response.

A second and seemingly opposed line of theory development pictures the subject as an active participant in the process of forming concepts. It asserts that an organism always entertains some hypothesis about the unknown concept. Each presented example and nonexample provides a test of a current hypothesis. Over a sequence of examples several hypotheses may be infirmed, but eventually the subject hits on the correct one and then the problem is solved.

In such a theory it is assumed that the subject does more than merely register incoming information. He uses it first as a check on his current hypothesis and then as a basis for modifying that hypothesis if it is incompatible with available evidence. While this type of theory originated with psychologists working outside the S-R Associationistic tradition, it is not totally inconsistent with modern versions in that tradition. Present-day Behaviorists and Associationists are quite comfortable with the notion of internal events and many have adopted the hypothesis-testing idea into their general theoretical frameworks.

Both lines of development have their merits. Both seem adequate as descriptions of certain facets of conceptual behavior. Both, of course, are far too simple to be true. Conceptual behavior is surely more complex than any currently popular theory can represent. But theories tend to stay just slightly in advance of empirical knowledge. Because we know so little, the theories too tend to be rather primitive. It is difficult to forecast the future, but we may find eventually that some combination of these basic ideas is more appropriate than either one taken alone; we will have more to say on this later.

We proceed now to consider some specific illustrations of theories which fit the S-R associational and the "hypothesis-testing" notions.

S-R Association Theories

Associationistic theories almost invariably picture concept formation as a complex form of discrimination learning; that is, as some elaboration of the processes of detecting and labeling discriminable aspects of stimulus patterns. The complication arises because concept problems, unlike "pure" discrimination problems, require that differential responses be associated only with certain "relevant" attributes of stimulus patterns.

There are two basic varieties of S-R theory, those which do and those which do not assign an essential role to internal, mediational processes intervening between stimulus input and response output. The critical issue is whether or not the conceptual behavior of an organism can be accounted for in terms of its relationship to properties of the external stimuli alone. If not, there must be other factors, that is, mediational factors, which are important in governing his overt behavior.

The decision on mediational processes is not a simple one. There are data obtained under some experimental circumstances which are explained quite easily and adequately by a nonmediated S-R theory. There are other data which seem to demand a mediational interpretation. We probably ought not to expect a simple answer. It is not unreasonable to believe that behavior is mediated under some circumstances and unmediated under others. Both notions may be correct, though bounded by the nature of the conceptual task and the behaving organism. It is worth mentioning here that mediational processes are often assumed to be verbal in substance. That is, they usually represent the use of words as symbols which code and integrate aspects of the external stimulus. Mediational explanations are then typically most useful in complex conceptual problems wherein an adult human being is the subject.

NONMEDIATED S-R INTERPRETATIONS: EARLY HULL.   Hull (1920) contributed to the study of conceptual behavior its first experimental methodology (the reception paradigm) independent of introspection. His procedure was devised to collect data on possible quantitative relationships between stimulus and response variables and to check on his (Behavioristic) analysis of concept formation. While mediational processes play an important role in Hull's later theorizing, his early position was stated in unelaborated S-R terms. To Hull concept formation was a discrimination process leading to the abstraction of an element (or combination of elements) common to a variety of stimulus patterns. He thought of it as a passive process wherein the common element became conditioned to the proper response. The general idea can be represented schematically in the accompanying sketch. Complex stimulus patterns are analyzable into elements, e_i. Certain elements, e_c, appear in all patterns assigned to a particular response. The dotted lines represent the learned associational linkages between e_c and the response "appropriate" to members of that concept.

Stimulus Patterns   Elements   Response

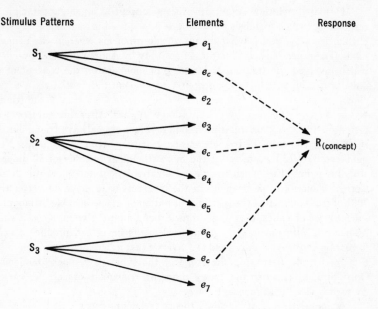

SKINNER.   A similar position was developed by Skinner (1953) as a part of his general behavior system. According to Skinner, if reinforcement (or reward) follows as a consequence of some response by an organism, all characteristics or elements of the stimulus effective at the time acquire a degree of control over that response. The amount of control grows with the repeated occurrences of response and reinforcement in the presence of the stimulus. The control developed is manifested whenever the previously reinforced stimulus appears, even if it occurs in or with other combinations of stimulus features. When behavior comes to be controlled by a few relevant stimulus features of a variety of otherwise dissimilar patterns, that behavior represents an abstraction and is called conceptual. "Squareness" is a concept familiar to most human beings because the response "square" (or some representative thereof) has been repeatedly reinforced when made in the presence of various stimulus patterns embodying the properties of a square. Somewhat more complicated but following the same lines of development are compound concepts, such as "large square" or large red square."

This interpretation also accounts reasonably well for the common observation that once a concept has been acquired it can be applied to new or unfamiliar stimuli. Only the existence (or nonexistence) of the conditioned stimulus characteristics is critical, for these determine how the subject will respond. The generality (or generalizability) of a concept to new stimuli is regulated only by those features involved in the original associational process.

HARLOW.   Harlow (1959) describes a concept as a general principle for responding (which he labels a learning set), acquired in the course of experiencing, learning, and solving many specific problems wherein the principle holds. The general idea is illustrated in a study by Andrew and Harlow (1948) which involved the training and testing of monkeys on the concept of triangularity. Subjects were trained first to respond differentially (in a two-choice task) to a single triangle and a single circle. Selection of the triangle was consistently followed by presentation of reward. After this, subjects were tested on 100 new pairs of stimuli, one of which was always triangular. On these trials, choice of the triangle was only slightly better than chance. Next, monkeys were trained to select the more triangular member of 50 different stimulus pairs, after which their generalization to 50 new pairs was tested. Correct choices (of the triangle) in the later test were made on better than 70% of trials indicating the (partial) formation of a generalizable "triangular" learning set or concept. Harlow argues that unlimited training on a single problem or with unchanging stimulus elements never can produce concept formation and *may* actually yield the inverse; that is, a reduction in generalization tendencies, narrowing the scope of the subject's response tendencies. Only through experiencing many different triangular objects in varying contexts will a "true" concept emerge.

A unique feature of Harlow's theory is the argument that learning sets are formed through a discrimination process whereby erroneous response tendencies are eliminated or inhibited. He contends that many stimulating factors operate on an organism on every trial in any problem. Suppression of error factors leaves the behavior of an organism under the control of the appropriate factor(s) only. The emphasis in this theory is on inhibition which is in one sense the antithesis of Hull's emphasis on the growth of an association. As we shall see later, error factors can be interpreted as erroneous hypothesis so that it is possible to recast Harlow's general notions to fit the basic structure of either an associational or a hypothesis-testing theory.

A MATHEMATICAL MODEL.   Bourne and Restle (1959) extended a theory of discrimination learning (Restle, 1957) to provide a quantitative account of data collected in concept identification problems. In this theory two underlying processes are assumed. Because certain (relevant) cues are consistently associated with a given (conceptual) response, they gradually become *conditioned* to the response. In this respect the theory is like Hull's and Skinner's. In addition, those (irrelevant) cues which are not consistently associated with any available response come to lose their effectiveness and are *adapted*. Conditioning and adaptation proceed regularly through the effect of informative feedback (which is assumed to serve the function of reinforcement). The rates of conditioning and adaptation are determined by the *proportion of relevant cues*. In other words, these processes proceed more rapidly as the number of valid cues to solution increases and/or the number of invalid cues decreases.

The probability that a subject will make the correct conceptual response on any trial of a problem is a function of the proportion of unadapted cues which up to that point have been conditioned to the response.

These statements may be formalized as follows: When the correct category response is signalled on any trial n, there is some probability that a relevant cue, k, will be conditioned. Allowing $C(k,n)$ to stand for the probability that k is conditioned on trial n we may write, by assumption, $C(k,n) = C(k,n-1)(1-\theta)+\theta$, where θ is a rate parameter determined by the proportion of relevant cues. Irrelevant cues are adapted with an independent but similarly derived probability. $A(k',n) = A(k',n-1)(1-\theta)+\theta$, where k' is some irrelevant cue.

The expressions for $C(k,n)$ and $A(k',n)$ are known as difference equations. They may be solved to provide an explicit formula determining the proportions of relevant cues which are conditioned and of irrelevant cues which are adapted on trial n, given only the rate parameter, θ, and the proportions of conditioned and adapted cues at the beginning of the trial sequence. With these expressions one may write the probability of a correct response on any trial n, $P(n)$ by forming the ratio of conditioned cues to total number of cues—conditioned plus unadapted irrelevant cues—which are still effective prior to trial n. Thus, $P(n)$ is shown to be:

$$P(n) = 1 - \frac{\frac{1}{2}(1-\theta)^{n-1}}{\theta + (1-\theta)^n}$$

The probability of an error response is simply $1-P(n)$, or

$$\frac{\frac{1}{2}(1-\theta)^{n-1}}{\theta + (1-\theta)^n}$$

Summing the expression, $1-P(n)$, over trials, the approximate predicted number of errors prior to solution of any such problem is:

$$E \simeq \frac{1}{2} + \frac{1}{2}\frac{\log \theta}{(1-\theta)\log (1-\theta)}$$

These equations describe performance in two-category problems with one relevant dimension. A more elaborate development is necessary for conjunctive tasks. Beyond this the theory is complicated by certain assumptions required by particular experiments. But, to discuss these would take us inappropriately into experimental results.

GIBSON.   One final example of nonmediated S-R theory will be presented briefly mainly because of its unique emphasis on generalization and discrimination processes. This theory, due initially to the work of Gibson (1940), grew mainly out of a concern for verbal paired-associates learning. Gibson

asserts that the basic problem for the subject in a paired-associate task is
to learn to make discriminations among the different stimulus items in a list.
The difficulty of this problem is largely a function of the degree of generalization (confusability?) among the items. The more generalization, the greater
the tendency on the part of a subject to give the same response learned or
associated with stimulus *x* to another similar item *x'*. Since the task requires
a different response for each stimulus, generalization impedes learning. The
gradient of stimulus generalization, note, is related to an underlying dimension
of stimulus similarity.

In concept learning, all positive instances of a given concept must be
paired with the same response and all negative instances with a different
response. These instances may be thought of as the stimuli of a paired-
associates list. When the positive instances (and/or negative instances) are
mutually similar the tendency to make the same response to each is great
and learning the list is relatively easy. But if there is much variability among
the positive (and/or negative) instances or if positive instances tend to be
similar to negative instances (or positive instances of a second concept),
learning may be difficult. These hypotheses were tested and largely confirmed
in an experiment reported by Baum (1954).

Several ways of looking at concept formation from an Associationistic
point of view have been described. While differing in some important respects,
they all agree that the stimulus groupings acquired in the process of forming
a concept are based on the discrimination of some property or properties
which sets apart examples from nonexamples of the concept. To many workers
in the area of conceptual behavior, such explanations seem inadequate to
handle certain problems wherein no element is common to all positive instances
of the concept. For example, what are the common attributes among a variety
of foods such as watermelon, cornflakes, and mashed potatoes? It has been
suggested that they provoke common "eating responses" which in turn
generate common stimulus sensations. But this possibility necessitates some
intervening link in the association between external stimulus and overt
response. Such a point of view has been developed by several theorists who
adhere basically to an S-R orientation. We proceed next to a description of
this more complicated form of S-R theory.

MEDIATED S-R THEORY: GENERAL OUTLINE.   While there are differences
of opinion among theorists, mediational interpretations of learning and
complex behavior have in common certain fundamental characteristics which
permit a general description rather than a series of individual treatments. A
mediational process is the device S-R psychologists use to represent important
behaviors which go on inside the organism. Mediational S-R theory focuses
on and attempts to explain internal (symbolic) activities which intervene
between external stimulus and overt response and which almost certainly
play an important role in governing those overt responses.

Most mediational accounts of conceptual behavior assume the basic validity of Hull's discrimination-abstraction theory. Concepts are learned through an associational process which links two or more stimuli with a common response. However, the common response in mediational theory has an internal as well as an external representation. Thus, rather than a direct linkage between physical stimuli and an overt act of behavior, there develops a complex (at least two-stage) chain of connections involving internal and external stimulus and response events.

Hull (1930) was the first theorist to use explicitly the construct of a mediator. According to him external stimulation may initiate in the organism an event called a "pure stimulus act." This is an internal response, functioning solely to produce additional stimulation which serves as a cue for further overt responding. This response is thought of as a miniaturized version (or fragment) of some form of overt behavior. One may represent any simple behavioral process as in the accompanying diagram:

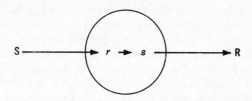

Here r is an internal "pure stimulus act" elicited by external stimulus, S, and which in turn generates internal stimulus s; s then produces overt behavior, R. As mentioned, the cue-producing function of r may itself be learned. Thus this notion allows for the entry of prior learning, stored in memory, into any new associational process.

Concept learning is often described as an acquired equivalence for a set of perceptibly different stimulus patterns. Within this theory the process is pictured as the acquisition of a common mediating response to the various patterns, which may be portrayed as in the accompanying diagram:

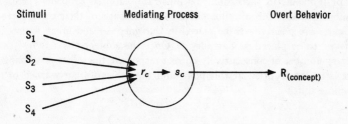

Thus conceptual behavior is described as a special mediated chain involving multiple converging linkages between Ss and r_c.

THE NEED FOR MEDIATIONAL PROCESSES.   The addition of internal (and typically unobservable) stimulus-response connections may appear at first to be an unnecessary elaboration of basic S-R theory. What important role do mediators play in behavior? Why is it necessary to postulate their existence at all? The answer to these questions is complex. First of all, it is clear that the internal mechanisms of an organism are not "silent." There are internal response mechanisms (muscles, glands, nerves) which are continuously active. Further, there are internal sensing mechanisms (specialized receptor cells, nerves) which are continuously alert to the internal environment just as the exterceptors (external receptors) are alert to the external environment. These activities are integrated complexly with the outward, ongoing behavior of an organism, which is probably reason enough to represent them in any theoretical account.

But further, there are the more "psychological" or phenomenological experiences of an organism, sometimes vaguely called symbolic behavior, which seem often to accompany and play an important role in concept formation. These events are difficult to get at, admittedly, and our evidence about them is primarily based on introspective or retrospective verbal reports. Nonetheless, they seem to be fairly regular. For example, it is common to experience some visual images while thinking about, say, the Washington Monument or the arrangement of furniture in one's home. Even more frequent perhaps is thinking in words when one attempts to reason out the possible solutions to a problem. Symbolic activities like these seem clearly to mediate various overt attempts at problem solving and necessitate some consideration and representation in a complete theory of conceptual behavior.

SOME EXPERIMENTAL EVIDENCE: SOLUTION SHIFTS.   The most compelling reason for introducing the notion of mediational processes into theory, of course, comes from experimental data and particularly from studies of conceptual problems which require solution shifts. We shall review some of these data in Chapter V; however, it is instructive to indicate the procedure and general results of solution shift studies at this point.

In the experiment the subject is required to solve two undimensional concept problems in succession. To illustrate, suppose Problem 1 requires the subject to sort the stimulus patterns on the basis of their color; that is, red figures are positive—to be placed in Category A—and green figures are negative—to be placed in Category B. Once the subject has attained some arbitrary number of consecutively correct responses, the solution is changed. There is no interruption at this point and the subject is not warned of the impending shift.

Two basic types of shift, called "reversal" and "nonreversal," are used. In a reversal shift the subject must learn to assign all formerly positive instances to Category B and all formerly negative instances to Category A. That is, the solution is precisely opposite to that required in Problem 1. Note, however, that the initially relevant dimension is still relevant in Problem 2. A nonreversal shift requires the subject to sort patterns in Problem 2 on the basis of some new relevant dimension. For example, after the shift, the subject may have to place all square figures in Category A and all triangles in Category B.

If concept formation is a process of associating physical stimulus attributes with overt category responses, the reversal condition should be more difficult than the nonreversal. The reasoning can be shown easily by means of a diagram:

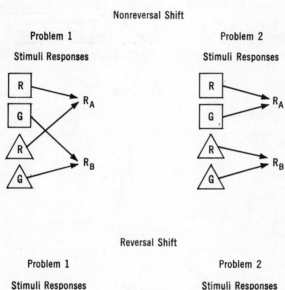

Nonreversal Shift

Problem 1	Problem 2
Stimuli Responses	Stimuli Responses

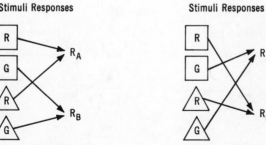

Reversal Shift

Problem 1	Problem 2
Stimuli Responses	Stimuli Responses

Note that 50% of the associations learned in Problem 1 continue to hold for Problem 2 in a nonreversal shift; that is, red squares are still placed in Category A, and green triangles in Category B. Only the categories for green square and red triangle are changed. In reversals, however, all Problem 1 associations must be changed in Problem 2; old associative connections must be extinguished and new ones conditioned. Thus if number of new associations to be formed (and/or old ones extinguished) is a measure of problem difficulty, reversal shifts should take longer to complete than nonreversals.

Whereas this prediction seems to hold when shift problems are given to preverbal children and lower organisms, just the opposite is true for adult human subjects (Kendler, 1960). That is, mature human beings find reversal shifts significantly easier than nonreversals. This inversion of problem difficulty is taken to imply the existence of certain mediational events in the behavior of adult human subjects which do not exist for less sophisticated organisms. Specifically, adults seem to learn both a mediating response of orienting or attending to a particular stimulus dimension (color in Problem 1) and overt category responses to identify any instance as positive or negative depending on the value it contains from the relevant dimension. In a reversal

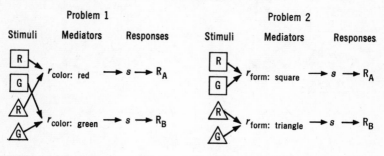

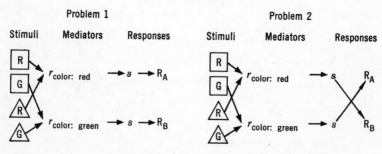

shift the mediating process remains unchanged since the relevant dimension is the same. In a nonreversal shift, however, a new mediation link must develop. Schematically, the process may be represented as in the diagram shown on the preceding page. Kendler, then, attributes the greater ease of reversal shifts for human subjects to the development of a mediator in Problem 1 which the subject may continue to use in Problem 2.

CHARACTERISTICS OF A MEDIATOR. Mediational theorists assume that internal (symbolic) behavior has essentially the same characteristics and is describable in essentially the same terms as overt behavior. But can we pin the mediator down any further? What are some possible concrete examples of it? In a concept problem with reversal and nonreversal shifts does the subject learn to orient physically (that is, some sensory-motor change) toward the relevant dimension; is the mediator some visual image; or is it a subaudible, verbal naming of the dimension? On the basis of several experiments showing changes in the relative difficulty of reversal and nonreversal shifts for lower animals and humans of various ages, Kendler and Kendler (1962) came to the conclusion that the mediator is probably verbal, and that internal verbalization is a self-generated, cue-producing behavior which guides orientation to the relevant attributes. Preverbal children and lower organisms, who perform better on nonreversal shifts, are surely capable of physical orientation, but they cannot vocalize either overtly or covertly.

The Kendlers stress the role of mediators in a learner's orientation toward key aspects of the stimuli. Osgood (1954) and others have emphasized the contribution of mediators to the meaning of stimulus objects. Prior associations of a given object carry its meaning and are represented internally as mediators. Here again the importance of verbal behavior is clear, since for the human adult, associates of a stimulus are coded and expressed largely in words. Forming concepts often can be seen as a process wherein the common meaning of various stimuli (mediators) is linked with some (possibly new) overt naming or category response. As a concrete example suppose a subject is given the task of learning to categorize a series of familiar objects (represented pictorially) such as a melon, a head of lettuce, a pork chop and so on, as positive instances and others, such as a house, an automobile and a tree, as negative. This is quite obviously a case where mediated meaning, based on earlier learning, would play an important function. "Food" is a strong associate (meaning) of all the positive items; the problem is solved once the new response—for example, "positive instance," "Category A," or some other label—is conditioned to this mediator.

CONCLUDING REMARKS. While it is impractical to present here the full complexity and implications of mediational theory, two additional points are worth noting. First, mediators provide the kind of building blocks from which so-called abstract and/or hierarchically arranged concepts can be formed. The most basic concepts seem to be those wherein simple stimulus attributes corresponding to physical dimensions are the fundamental elements. Mediational representations of these groupings can be combined complexly so as to produce concepts with no physical referents or instances; that is, concepts defined solely in the abstract with words. Theoretically, mediationally represented concepts can be combined and arranged into higher-order, more inclusive groupings interminably except for limitations on the intellect of the individual dealing with them.

Second, mediators provide the mechanism in S-R theory for interaction between internal and external events. These internalized habits generate stimulation which combines and competes with environmental stimulation for the control of overt behavior in present circumstances. The mediator is the means by which prior learning (or memory for previous events) enters into present behavior.

Theories Based on Hypothesis Testing

Associational theories picture learning as a passive, somewhat automatic stamping-in of connections between stimulus events and responses. In contrast the type of theory we call hypothesis testing views the organism as an "active" learner. He is assumed to possess some selectivity. He operates in important ways on his environment. First, he may not respond to all available stimulus features but rather select and attend to only certain aspects which, on the basis of a hypothesis, are considered relevant. Second, the subject decides upon and executes a response, in conformance with the hypothesis, which serves as a test of its adequacy. Typically, such a theory views any possible associational process, say, between critical stimulus features and the correct hypothesis (or the responses which implement that hypothesis) as trivial. While such associations may develop, they are merely a by-product of selection and test routines. Furthermore, because of the nature of these routines, associations are presumed to develop quickly, perhaps on a single trial, if the hypothesis can be proved all at once. The important learning does not involve S-R associations but rather the acquisition of knowledge, recognition, and "understanding" of a principle required by the task.

Hypothesis-testing theories purport to account for much the same domains of behavior as do the more traditional interpretations. An early example of such a theory can be found in the writings of Krechevsky (1932) who produced some important and convincing evidence on hypothesis-like behavior in rats learning simple two-choice discrimination tasks. In this problem the animal is rewarded for making one of two approach responses depending on which of two stimulus patterns (for example, triangle or square) is presented. In Krechevsky's data it seemed clear that at least some animals were testing hypotheses based on the spatial position of stimuli or the alternation of responses as well as on form differences.

Levine (1959, 1963) has adopted certain features of Krechevsky's analysis and coupled them with Harlow's (1959) error factor notions so as to produce a more explicit model of hypothesis behavior in somewhat more complicated circumstances. Like Harlow, Levine assumes that many environmental factors compete for the subject's attention in any situation. Problem solving consists primarily of testing and eliminating hypotheses based on all factors which are more powerful than the correct one. Once the correct factor is attended to, no further errors are made and the problem is solved. Levine has provided a statistical technique for evaluating the potency of various factors or hypotheses and for making predictions about performance.

As was the case with S-R accounts, hypothesis theories were first developed and evaluated in the context of experimental tasks, like discrimination learning, which are simpler than conceptual problems. But their usefulness transcends these simpler situations, and several attempts have been made to extend these basic notions. We shall look at three foremost examples.

HYPOTHESES, STRATEGIES, AND DECISION MAKING. Bruner, Goodnow, and Austin (1956) reported a thorough theoretical and empirical analysis of many aspects of human conceptual behavior. They describe the processes of forming and utilizing concepts as a series of decisions. The subject is presumed to begin any problem by deciding on some tentative hypothesis which may attribute importance (that is, relevance) to one, some, or all of the dimensions which vary within the population of stimuli to be categorized. The hypothesis, here, is some statable combination of attributes, such as "all *large red squares* belong to the positive class," which guides the category placement of any stimulus instance. Upon learning the outcome of each category response, the subject is required to make further decisions. If the hypothesis is wrong he must decide how to change it; even if the hypothesis works on a given occasion the subject may decide to reduce or augment its scope (that is, drop or add some attribute or attributes). Thus, conceptual behavior, in general, is looked upon as a sequential decision-making activity, in which later decisions are contingent upon earlier ones.

The uniqueness of this approach and analysis is its emphasis upon and determination of certain regularities in the decision-making, hypothesis-testing procedures of human subjects. In the experiments by Bruner *et al.*, subjects followed definite *strategies* or plans of attack on conceptual problems. We shall provide here a simple example. A problem, based on a conjunction of two relevant attributes, is constructed and presented under conditions of the previously described selection paradigm. Suppose the concept is "two squares" ($2\square$). Suppose further that the basic stimulus population has four dimensions, color, form, number, and size, each with three values, and consists of (3^4) 81 different patterns. The experimenter designates one pattern, .

say 2MG□ (two medium-sized green squares), as positive. In accord with task requirements, then, the subject must offer his best guess of the concept, and if wrong, must select some stimulus pattern from the population to gain further information toward solution. (Note that, in general, the subject will not know in the beginning how many relevant attributes the concept has.) One strategy which is used frequently, especially by subjects with some degree of prior training and/or sophistication, is called *conservative focusing*. Here, the subject adopts as his first tentative hypothesis all attributes of the positive (focus) instance designated by the experimenter. After only one (positive) instance, this hypothesis represents the best available guess about the concept, for any or all of the attributes of this instance *may* be relevant. Thus, in the example, 2MG□ is the subject's first hypothesis. The subject then proceeds to select a stimulus which differs from the first on only *one* dimension, say, 1MG□. If the attribute changed (1 in place of 2) is irrelevant then this instance will be positive; if the changed attribute is relevant this instance will be negative. These outcomes follow from the definition of conjunctive concepts which require the joint presence of all relevant attributes (and only relevant attributes) in positive instances. In the example, since the concept is 2□, 1MG□ is a negative instance. Upon gaining this information, the subject knows 2 is a relevant attribute and he maintains the tentative hypothesis, 2MG□. The next instance selected should differ from the first in one other attribute; thus the subject may select 2LG□. Since this instance is positive, the subject now knows that size is unimportant and may reduce his tentative hypothesis to 2G□.

If this strategy for selecting stimuli and revising hypotheses is followed consistently the subject will arrive at problem solution in a minimal number of decisions and tests. It is well to note the efficiency of this plan of attack. At each stage the subject is left with a hypothesis which represents all that he has learned about relevant and irrelevant attributes up to that point. It is, in a sense, a composite hypothesis in that it embodies all subhypotheses which are still tenable. Many solutions are possible at the outset; given that 2MG□ is a positive instance, 2M, MG□, M, 2□, and so forth are all possible solutions. Adopting 2MG□ (all attributes) as a first guess means that all reasonable hypotheses are entertained. Similarly, when M is eliminated as an irrelevant attribute, 2G□ is a composite hypothesis which contains all solutions which have not been infirmed. Thus the strategy is quite efficient if only because it reduces the memory requirements which would otherwise be imposed by the task.

Several points remain to be clarified with respect to the position taken by Bruner *et al.* First, conservative focusing is only one of several strategies used by subjects for making decisions and testing hypotheses. Furthermore, some subjects, particularly unsophisticated ones, do not follow any particular strategy to the letter. Rather they may approximate conservative focusing, while making some mistakes and showing considerable variation.

Second, and related to the first point, is the fact that subjects usually do not formulate a definite strategy in any way approaching the deliberate manner implied in the foregoing description. These regularities can be detected in response sequences, although the subject may not or cannot verbalize it. In other words, a subject seems often to use a strategy in a more intuitive than formal way.

Third, strategies are not to be thought of as fixed and inalterable. They depend on a variety of factors determined by the problem, and the conditions under which it is solved, and are subject to continual modification. Presumably, then, learning is an important factor in strategic behavior. How strategies are learned, however, is a question only further research can answer. One reasonable lead for such research comes from the studies of learning set formation, for the strategies discussed by Bruner *et al.*, though typically befitting more complex problems than "oddity," may be interpreted, like Harlow's learning sets, as generic behavioral principles which are applicable in a variety of problematic situations. Just as the oddity learning set directs the subject to choose the unique member of any stimulus array, conservative focusing directs a sequence of stimulus selections necessary to pinpoint some conjunctive combination of relevant attributes. Both devices are "independent" of the particular stimulus features within which a given problem is cast. Both implement the utilization of some rule (oddity, conjunction, or otherwise).

An "information-processing" model. Hovland (1952) and later Hunt (Hovland and Hunt, 1960; Hunt, 1962) developed the rudiments of what has been called an information-processing model of conceptual behavior. This theory attributes to the concept learner certain primitive or basic procedures (called information-processing units) for receiving, organizing, and interpreting stimulus and feedback inputs from the environment in such a way as to define a conceptual grouping. The idea is to include in the model a minimal repertoire of procedures sufficient for the model to mimic or simulate the behavior of real subjects.

The initial construction of the model is based on the results of many available experiments. Assuming the basic adequacy of a hypothesis-testing description of conceptual behavior, the model has to have one or more procedures for generating and testing tentative solutions. The procedure adopted directs the model to "attend to" the positive instances (of some unknown concept) presented to it, with the aim of discovering attributes of these instances which are common. Utilization of "positive focusing" was indicated by the research of Bruner *et al.*, which often showed a tendency for human subjects to explore carefully the implications of each positive instance while virtually ignoring negative instances. (Actually, the Hunt-Hovland model adopts a modified positive-focusing procedure, which they call conditional focusing. This allows the model to solve nonconjunctive concepts wherein all positive instances do not share the same common attributes. Thus, the model attacks these problems as conjunctions *with exceptions*.)

The model builds a description of the correct concept in the form of a tree of decisions. Each nodal point or decision point in the tree considers one relevant dimension of each successive instance, leading on to one branch if a certain attribute is present in the instance and to the other branch if it is missing. The complexity of the final tree, that is, the number of decision points it contains, depends both on the number of relevant dimensions and number of exceptions to the common attributes description of a concept.

The model constructed by Hunt and Hovland is far more complex than can be presented here and the interested reader is referred to Hunt's book (1962) for a complete résumé. We shall consider only a few additional points. First of all, the model can be realized as a computer program so that predictions and complex simulations of real data can be produced both efficiently and rigorously. Second, this theory is one of the few which makes any real attempt to account for the learning and utilization of concepts based on rules other than conjunction. This must be viewed as an important step, for real-life concepts of disjunctive, relational, and other varieties are too common to be ignored.

The model is, however, tacit on some very important issues and surely requires a great deal of expansion to approach completeness. The single most important issue yet to be resolved is the question of where information processing units come from. Are they learned, as such? Are they analyzable into elementary S-R associations? Or are they innate abilities? Two other questions (also recognized by Hunt, 1962, see p. 240), have to do with (a) the veridicality and degree of memory for previous instances afforded the model and (b) the way in which complicated transfer effects from one problem to the next—so common in human conceptual behavior—can be simulated. We can expect important insights into these problems in the near future.

A MATHEMATICAL MODEL OF HYPOTHESIS TESTING. The positions espoused by both Bruner *et al.*, and Hunt, while elaborate and quite descriptive, are actually not intended by the authors to serve as formal theories of conceptual behavior. Though they involve certain assumptions about underlying processes, neither is developed to a point which allows many deductive or predictive possibilities. They remain largely as post hoc descriptions of experimental data. Restle (1962), on the other hand, has developed a simpler, but more explicit quantitative theory of hypothesis testing which supplies at least the rudiments of a rigorous theory of conceptual behavior.

Restle assumes that any problematic situation gives rise to a pool of hypotheses. Presumably each hypothesis could be identified with one or more stimulus attributes, though in principle there is no need to specify them in this way. Most of these hypotheses are incorrect in one of two senses; either they will always lead the subject to make a wrong response, as for example when the hypothesis reverses the classes of positive and negative instances, or they produce wrong responses at chance level, as when some irrelevant attribute forms the basis for a hypothesis. One or more hypotheses from the pool are correct; that is, correspond to the solution. If and when one of these hypotheses is adopted no errors will be made in classifying the stimulus pattern.

Hypotheses from the basic pool may, according to Restle's theory, be selected and tested in one of three ways each of which amounts to a particular strategy. (1) The subject may select and test hypotheses one at a time. He begins by selecting a hypothesis at random from the pool. This hypothesis is held until an error (incorrect category response) is made, after which it is returned to the pool and a new hypothesis is chosen. The procedure is continued until, by random choice, the correct hypothesis is sampled. Since this hypothesis never leads to error, the problem is solved. (2) According to the second strategy the subject begins by considering all possible hypotheses at once. Given the first stimulus, some proportion of hypotheses will indicate "positive instance" and others "negative instance." The response made by the subject is determined by the larger of these two proportions. If the response is correct all hypotheses leading to the contrary response are eliminated, and the subject begins to close in on the correct hypothesis. By a process of elimination the subject ends with the single correct hypothesis. (3) The third strategy is a compromise between the first two. The subject presumably begins with a sample greater than one but less than all, from the pool of hypotheses. Again the process is one of elimination until the correct hypothesis in the sample is located or the sample is exhausted. In the latter case, the subject must return to the pool for a new sample. It can be shown that Strategies 1 and 2 above are special cases (both behaviorally and mathematically) of Strategy 3; in Case 1 the sample size is one, and in Case 2 the sample size is the entire pool.

One surprising outcome of Restle's mathematical analysis is the fact that each strategy leads to the same expectations in the data. That is, though formally different, the three models generate the same predictions. Consider briefly how these predictions are realized. We shall develop this only for Strategy 1, wherein the subject selects and tests one hypothesis at a time.

Suppose that in the pool of hypotheses the proportion of relevant ones (there may, of course, be only one) is r. The probability of sampling one of these prior to Trial 1 is r; thus, some proportion, r, of subjects working on the same problem will solve without any errors simply because they choose the correct hypothesis at the outset. Generally speaking—because r is smaller than $1-r$, the proportion of incorrect hypotheses—many more subjects will make at least one error. What is the probability of making *exactly* one error before solving the problem? For this to be the case, the subject must sample first a wrong hypothesis, reject it on the occasion of an error, and then choose the correct hypothesis. The probability of this event sequence is $(1-r)r$, or the product of independent probabilities representing an incorrect and a correct hypothesis selection. In general, if we wish to know the probability of making exactly n errors, we evaluate $(1-r)^n r$.

Usually, what we will want to evaluate for any experimental problem is the expected number of errors; that is, how many errors will a group of subjects make on the average. To obtain this expectation, we consider the fact that the frequency distribution or probability distribution of errors is known mathematically as the exponential distribution; that is, $P\{E = n\} = r(1-r)^n$. This distribution has a well-known expectation; namely, $E = \dfrac{1-r}{r}$. The average number of errors (E) will be the ratio of $1-r$, the proportion of incorrect hypotheses, to r, the proportion of correct hypotheses—*if the theory holds*. Thus, in order to predict the average number of errors for any problem, all we need to know is r.

Without making a strict identification of each hypothesis with some distinguishable facet of the problematic situation, it is impossible to "count" the number of correct and incorrect hypotheses available to the subject. The typical evaluative procedure is to "calibrate" problems by using the experimental data from one or more control conditions of a study to obtain an estimate of r. Then the remaining conditions of the study are "predicted," using the obtained r plus other theoretical considerations pertaining to the procedural differences among conditions.

Restle's theory gives a very clear and accurate account of many quantitative details of experiments on simple conceptual behavior. It should be recognized, however, that the theory is far from complete, and it is certainly not universally accepted. Its predictions are, perforce, statistical and not deterministic. Further, the theory provides no means of predicting relationships among the specific hypotheses tested on successive trials. That hypotheses are to some extent contingent on one another seems clear from the results of Bruner *et al.*, although Restle's theory would have them independent. But Restle's development is no mean accomplishment; it does yield as good or better predictions than any competitor. It cannot be rejected completely because it sometimes fails to reflect known facets of the data.

Some General Comments

Associational theories visualize concept learning as a process wherein new linkages are gradually developed, either between distinguishable features of an external stimulus and an overt response or, somewhat more complexly, among a chain of stimulus and response events, some of which are internal to the organism. Hypothesis-testing theories assert that the linkages, if there are any, either already exist or are formed instantaneously and that the basic problem for the subject is discovering which linkage (hypothesis) works. The theories seem to be different and yet they are not entirely incompatible. It may be that an element of truth exists in both and that each "works" in certain problematic situations.

Consider, first, that hypothesis-testing theories almost demand that the subject have some prior experience relevant to the problem before he begins. Somehow it seems only reasonable that the subject must have seen and differentiated potentially important stimulus attributes before he can cast them in the form of hypotheses. Furthermore, although the nature of a subject's hypothesis may be left unspecified by theory, it is likely that a hypothesis involving two or more attributes (as would be required by all but simple unidimensional concepts) is based on some prior learning of rules for combining attributes. If this is true the same argument holds (even more strongly) for such things as strategies. We have seen that strategies are modifiable and not innate modes of behavior. In sum, it is probable that hypothesis-testing and more general strategic behavior is a relatively sophisticated kind of performance, not likely to characterize the behavior of young, naïve, or stupid subjects.

It may be that hypothesis testing characterizes the preformance of subjects with at least some minimal backlog of training which is transferable to new conceptual problems. This backlog may very well derive, at least initially, from the gradual acquisition of associations among stimulus attributes and responses. The naïve subject will have to learn some stimulus discriminations and responses for the discriminated attributes. Given these associations, particularly if they have been internalized in some way so as to serve as mediational linkages, the subject has the raw material for forming simple hypotheses. Any new problem which has as its solution one of these preformed associations, e.g., □ → "square," may be solved rapidly by the subject, as if by hypothesis testing, for the required categorization involves merely the association, □ → "positive instance" which is mediated by the well-learned label "square." But if the same problem was given to a naïve subject—one who had not learned the association between □ and "square" —or if a formally identical problem was constructed but with unfamiliar nonsense forms such that ⫝ must be placed in the positive category, we might very well observe gradual nonhypothesis-like learning, for truly new associations, unmediated by any relevant prior learning, would be formed.

It is possible to think of nonmediated S-R, mediated S-R, and hypothesis-testing theories as representing some sort of continuum of behavioral sophistication. Indeed, mediational and hypothesis-testing theories seem to differ mainly in technical language, and except for the manner in which internal processes are initiated—mediators through some stimulus cuing event and hypotheses by a subject-determined selection process—are often directly translatable. The theories are not necessarily incompatible. In fact, conflicts seem to arise only when a theorist, committed to a single position, insists that his theory holds for all behavior no matter what the circumstances.

OTHER THEORIES

No pretense at an exhaustive listing and description of psychological theories relevant to conceptual behavior is made here. Space permits at best a sampling, and we have elected to discuss only those theories which (*a*) are reasonably explicit, (*b*) enjoy some degree of current popularity and are the subject of recent experimentation, and (*c*) illustrate one of the two theoretical main streams, either associational or hypothesis-testing.

Perhaps the most glaring omission from this discussion, which many readers may recognize and which, therefore, deserves special comment is the theoretical work of Piaget (for example, 1957). Piaget's contribution to and influence on the general psychology of the human thinking is appreciable. But it is difficult to accommodate his position within this discussion. The facts that (*a*) its support derives almost exclusively from Piaget's own naturalistic observations, (*b*) its domain is far broader than our delimitation of conceptual behavior, and (*c*) it diverges widely from conventional American theory leads us to minimize its consideration here and in the pages which follow.

IV

Task Variables

HAVING CONSIDERED SOME of the procedural and theoretical issues, the next step in this survey is to look in more detail at the results of experimentation. Prior to 1950 there was a dearth of factual evidence on human conceptual processes; a recent upsurge of interest, however, has provided now a respectable body of knowledge. From the many ways in which this information can be organized, we have chosen a breakdown according to classes of functional relationships. In this chapter we shall deal with task variables and their effects on performance, and in Chapter V, we shall take up conditions more closely identified with the problem solver; that is, organismic variables.

The aim of this presentation is twofold. The first is to provide the reader with a review of the existing empirical knowledge in the area. Second, we intend to point out the theoretical implications of certain experiments. In this way additional evaluative evidence for theoretical ideas in Chapter III can be provided.

In this chapter we deal with an array of factors which can be called "task variables." These variables have to do with the ecological conditions under which the subject must work to produce solutions to conceptual problems. As examples, we shall discuss characteristics of the stimulus materials to be categorized and aspects of responses which the subject is required to make. It is difficult to draw a firm line between task variables and other conditions which will be discussed elsewhere. To illustrate, when an experiment compares concept formation under conditions which either do or do not allow the subject to keep track of previously given stimulus information with paper and pencil, is it a study of memory (presumably an organismic factor) or a study of stimulus availability (presumably a task factor)? We make no attempt to answer such questions. The classification of variables used here is admittedly arbitrary. Our primary purpose is to relate the available evidence in concise and understandable fashion and not to quibble about the definitional ambiguities.

RESPONSE VARIABLES

Recall from Chapter I that three fundamentally different response requirements have commonly been imposed on subjects in conceptual problems. In the reception paradigm the subject usually makes a category response to each stimulus. In the selection paradigm each trial may necessitate that the subject select one of a large number of stimulus patterns in order to gain information about the concept. Still a third type of response appears to be useful within both paradigms. The subject may be required periodically to guess what the concept is; that is, to formulate a hypothesis on each trial or after each block of n trials. From these various responses a number of performance measures can be derived. For example, certain regularities in trial-by-trial stimulus selections and hypotheses can be interpreted as a reflection of underlying strategies used by the subject. We shall be concerned with the informativeness and adequacy of these measures in the following section. We shall also summarize some experiments in which variations in response requirements affect certain aspects of problem solving.

Measures of Performance

Probably the most common measures of performance in conceptual problems are number of trials, number of incorrect (or correct) responses, and time to solution. All three provide essentially the same performance index. In the first place, correlations between them are invariably high, ranging around .90 (for example, Bourne, 1957; Byers, 1963). If errors are large in number, trials and time to solution are found also to be large. Further, it is almost always the case that these measures are affected in the same way by important independent variables of experiments. For example, Bulgarella and Archer (1962) reported that errors, trials, and time increase in parallel fashion with task difficulty. In general, then, the outcome of most experiments can be summarized in terms of any one of these measures alone.

Time, total errors, and total trials to solution, along with certain other indices, such as the proportion of subjects in an experimental group who solve (or fail) a problem, are measures of over-all performance; they provide little or no detailed information on how the subject attains solution. In most cases it is reasonable to assume that an independent variable which affects speed of problem solving also influences the sequence of behaviors leading to it. Nearly always, we may consider the subject's individual overt responses to be related systematically to and indicative of his strategy or plan of attack on the problem. Thus, we can expect to find in many experimental reports the use of detailed analyses of response sequences in an effort to get at the more precise characteristics of performance.

These finer analyses take various forms and are difficult to summarize.

Often they explore the contingencies within trial-by-trial category responses, hypotheses, or stimulus selections. Some analyses aim at a determination of possible interrelationships among types of responses. Because of their complexity and diversity these analytic techniques are best discussed within the context of appropriate experiments. To illustrate, however, we shall look again briefly at the pioneering work on strategies for conceptual problems by Bruner, Goodnow, and Austin (1956).

These researchers inspected stimulus selections and verbalized hypotheses to detect systematic, sequential behaviors of subjects. In conjunctive problems Bruner *et al.* found evidence of at least four specifiably different plans or strategies used by subjects. Probably the most efficient of these, considering limitations on human memory, is *conservative focusing*. This strategy calls for an initial hypothesis containing all attributes of a positive instance, which the subject then refines in the direction of the concept by selecting successive stimuli which differ in only one attribute from the initial focus instance. Any dimension which, when changed in value, does not affect the positive status of the instance is irrelevant and may be dropped from the hypothesis. In this way, with a sufficient number of stimulus selections and tests, the true concept is determined.

Particularly under conditions which emphasize the importance of rapid solutions, some subjects follow a strategy called *focus gambling*. This procedure differs from conservative focusing mainly in the way stimuli are selected for test. Here the subject changes two (or more) attributes of the focus instance when he selects a stimulus. For example, given the positive focus 2MG□, the subject may next choose 1SG□. If the subject is fortunate in his stimulus selections, focus gambling can pay handsome dividends. Suppose the concept is G□. Selection of 1SG□, a positive instance, tells the subject at once that number and size are irrelevant dimensions and limits the remaining possible concepts to three, G, □, or G□. Two stimulus selections would be required to gain the same amount of information by conservative focusing. There is an element of risk involved in focus gambling, however, and therein lies the reason for its name. If either or both of the changed attributes, 2 and M, are relevant, 1SG□ is a negative instance. Its selection does not provide definitive information; the subject will have to choose additional instances, say 1MG□ and 2SG□, to determine which of the originally changed attributes is or are important. In this case the strategy will require three stimulus selections, as opposed to two, for conservative focusing. Whether the subject will "take a chance" on focus gambling depends, as we have indicated, on several factors, particularly the degree of pressure to solve the problem in a hurry; that is, with a minimal number of stimulus selections.

Both focus gambling and conservative focusing strategies are based on testing the relevance of stimulus attributes present in a positive instance. Bruner *et al.* also observed two distinguishable strategies reminiscent of the hypothesis-testing procedures assumed in Restle's model (1962). They called these *successive-* and *simultaneous-scanning* strategies. Here, the subject begins by adopting, tentatively, as hypotheses one (successive) or more (simultaneous) of the possible concepts which are consistent with the first positive instance. For example, given 2MG☐ as positive, the subject may decide to test the hypothesis, 2G; when infirmed on some trial, this guess is rejected and some other possibility is chosen to replace it. The process continues until the correct concept is discovered. Alternatively, the subject may assume several or all possible concepts as hypotheses (for example, 2, 2M, 2G☐) at the outset, gradually eliminating incorrect possibilities with each stimulus selection. Both strategies put an undue strain on memory. To use successive scanning efficiently, the subject must remember not only what hypotheses he has tested and rejected on earlier trials but also the various instances which have been encountered so that new hypotheses can be chosen to be consistent with them. To use simultaneous scanning, the subject must be able to keep track of a large array of possible solutions, at least on the early trials. Both factors probably exceed the limits of human memory in all but the simplest concept problems. On all counts, both strategies are inferior to conservative focusing (although logically they are no less efficient).

Two somewhat different strategies were detected in experiments using the reception paradigm. Here the subject has no opportunity to select stimuli and must rely on an experimentally regulated flow of information. Subjects' verbalized hypotheses showed evidence of either a *partist* or a *wholist* approach. The wholist subject adopts as his initial hypothesis all attributes of the first (positive) instance. He then proceeds, as the focuser, to modify that initial guess in the light of information provided in the successive stimulus instances. The partist subject differs only in that his initial hypothesis contains some (one or more) but not all attributes of the first positive instance. The factors accounting for this difference are obscure but seem to have more to do with the intellect and sophistication of the subject than with the nature of the task.

These then are some of the strategies subjects are known to use in conceptual problems. There are surely others which remain to be discovered. First of all, we know that these strategies are largely limited to problems with a conjunctive (or unidimensional) solution. Hunt's work (1962) shows that modifications in method of attack are called for when the solution is based on some other rule. Second, different, though no less systematic, behaviors would be appropriate in other kinds of conceptual problems, such as rule learning, in which the identification of relevant attributes is not a requirement. But, our aim here has not been to provide an exhaustive listing of systematic behaviors in conceptual tasks. Rather, we sought only to illustrate how detailed analysis of trial-by-trial responses can yield a much more penetrating understanding of conceptual behavior, and the variables which affect it, than can an inspection of superficial, over-all measures, such as time and trials to solution.

Some Relationships Between Category Responses and Hypotheses

Bourne (1965) reported an experiment, using the reception paradigm, in which the subject was required to name a category and to give his current hypothesis in response to each of a series of stimuli. This procedure permitted the use of measures such as trials and errors to problem solution as over-all efficiency criteria for various aspects of the subject's hypothesis selections and hypothesis changes. Subjects with a poorer over-all record differed from the better subjects in the following significant ways. (a) They more often failed to shift or change their hypotheses after making an incorrect category response. Obviously, an incorrect category response can be made only if the subject entertains an incorrect hypothesis. Failure to change this hypothesis when indicated means that additional category errors will be made. (b) They made changes in their hypotheses which were less consistent with information provided not only by the immediate stimulus but also by stimuli presented earlier in the sequence of trials. (c) They tended to make more complex changes in their hypotheses. The majority of changes made by the better subjects were changes either in size of hypothesis, that is, adding to or dropping an attribute from the hypothesis, or changes in composition, that is, replacing one attribute of the hypothesis with another. Rarely were changes in both size and composition made simultaneously by these subjects. On the other hand, the less efficient subjects made more complex and often seemingly erratic or haphazard hypothesis changes. (d) They tended to adopt an initial hypothesis which embodied fewer attributes of the first positive stimulus pattern than did the better subjects. This finding suggests that more efficient subjects are more likely to use a wholist (focusing) strategy, similar to that observed by Bruner et al. (1956), which leads to the identification of relevant attributes through the systematic elimination of irrelevant ones. The latter finding was replicated and extended in another study (Bourne, 1963b) in which a significant positive correlation between over-all performance and size of initial hypothesis was demonstrated.

The results of this experiment indicate that the better than average learner is one who starts with a hypothesis which uses most or all of the stimulus attributes. Further, he changes his hypothesis at the appropriate time; that is, after it has led him to make an incorrect category response. Finally, the changes he makes are by and large simpler, more systematic, and more consistent with available information than are the changes of the poorer problem solver. These findings, while not entirely unexpected, are useful for several reasons. First of all, they provide an important check on the relationships between measures based on two basically different types of performance, verbalized hypotheses and category responses. There is a degree of consistency in these measures, in that one can identify the quality of performance from both. Beyond this the results attest to the importance of measures and detailed analyses of hypothesis behavior in the development of a complete description and understanding of human conceptual functioning.

A Comparison of the Selection and Reception Paradigms

As noted, a major difference between experimental procedures used in the study of conceptual behavior is based on whether the sequence of stimuli is determined by the experimenter or the subject. The majority of studies have adopted the paradigm in which the experimenter arranges the stimulus order. However, the selection paradigm, which permits the subject to test instances in the order he prefers, has seen increasingly more frequent usage. Noting the differences in response requirements, Huttenlocher (1962) performed an experiment comparing the difficulty of solving problems under these two paradigms.

Subjects of the selection group were allowed to construct a stimulus pattern for test on each trial by placing each of two (or three) distinctly shaped stimulus objects such that either its black or its white side was showing. Thus, the basic stimulus population had two (or three) dimensions, each with two values, black and white. One dimension only was relevant to solution. After each pattern was constructed a signal from the experimenter indicated whether or not it was a positive instance. The subject was allowed to construct a series of patterns until enough information had been provided logically to determine the concept. At this point the subject was required to indicate his hypothesis. Note that this procedure differed somewhat from the usual selection paradigm in that the array of possible stimulus patterns was not available to the subject for continuous inspection. Here the construction of each new pattern required the removal of the previous one.

Each subject in the selection group had a matched counterpart in the reception group. The paired reception subject was shown by the experimenter a series of instances which was the same as that constructed by his counterpart in the selection group. Thus the two matched subjects had exactly the same information, presented in exactly the same order, from which to arrive at the concept. In a series of 12 successive concept problems, significantly more correct solutions were attained by subjects in the reception group. Huttenlocher attributed the difference in performance to the added necessity for selection subjects to plan and to construct the stimulus pattern on each trial. These additional requirements presumably interfered (by distraction) with the subject's retention, interpretation, and/or use of concept-relevant information. While the result indicates that better over-all performance is likely to occur with the reception paradigm, two qualifications are worth noting. First, the subjects in this experiment were seventh grade children—adults may be less distracted by the requirements of selection. Second, even if performance does suffer somewhat in the selection paradigm, this technique still provides information on the strategies of conceptual behavior which is unavailable in the reception paradigm. Thus, except for those research problems where maximally efficient performance is an absolute necessity, experimenters have no reason to discontinue use of the selection procedure.

Complexity Factors in a Category Response System

In the reception paradigm the subject must use some arbitrary system of categories for responding. If only a single concept is to be formed or identified the characteristics of this response system, for example, saying "plus" or "yes" for positive instances and "minus" or "no" for negative instances, probably have little or no effect on the difficulty of the problem. There are, however, many studies which require the subject to learn not one but several concepts concurrently. Performance in this more complicated task is affected markedly by the fact that each of the several concepts must be associated with a unique response. There are at least two ways in which such a requirement may add to the over-all complexity of a task. First, if the responses to be made are unfamiliar or meaningless the subject will have to learn what they are and how to produce them before he can perform adequately in the task. Some experimenters (for example, Baum, 1954) have used nonsense syllables, such as DAX or VEC, as concept labels which almost certainly imposes the necessity of response learning on the subject. Second, as the number of unique conceptual groupings to be learned in a problem increases, so does the number of new associations between concepts and labels. The formation of these associations is largely a matter of rote learning and may have little or nothing to do with the identification of concepts. Yet, before the subject can display his knowledge of the concepts, he must learn the associated labels prescribed by the task.

Richardson and Bergum (1954) showed that an appreciable amount of time in a concept-learning problem is invested by subjects in the learning of responses and their arbitrary assignment to these concepts. In their study the subjects learned to respond with the appropriate letter of the alphabet when an instance (geometric design) of any of nine concepts was presented. The task was divided into three parts: (1) identifying and naming all dimensions and levels of the stimuli, (2) discovering the relevant dimensions, and (3) associating the correct letter with each concept. They found that the percentage of total trials required on the average in each stage was 7%, 10%, and 83%, respectively. This result suggests that nonconceptual response requirements can contribute significantly to task difficulty, especially in multiconcept problems.

Providing evidence on a closely related question are two experiments which explored number of relevant dimensions as a variable in concept identification. Both experiments compared the difficulty of unidimensional problems (one relevant dimension) with conjunctive problems having two and three relevant dimensions. Bulgarella and Archer (1962) required subjects to sort stimulus patterns into two categories, that is, positive and negative instances, on the basis of one, two, or three relevant attributes. Walker and Bourne (1961) manipulated the same variable in such a way that number of response categories increased with number of relevant dimensions. Whereas the unidimensional concept had the same two-category form, conjunctive problems with two and three relevant dimensions required the subject to sort stimulus patterns into four and eight categories, respectively. In other words, the conjunctive problems contained as separate categories all possible combinations of the two values on the relevant dimensions. The difference between the two experiments which concerns us here is a matter of response system complexity. Problems used in these studies are comparable in stimulus

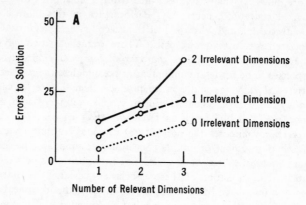

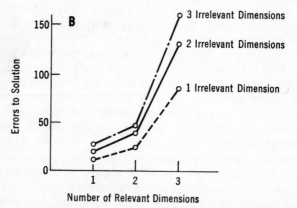

Figure 4. A comparison of the results of experiments by (A) Bulgarella and Archer (1962) and (B) Walker and Bourne (1961). Performance gets worse as number of relevant dimensions increases. However, the trend is essentially linear in Panel A and clearly nonlinear in Panel B. Trend differences probably can be assigned to response complexity (see text). Note that the effect of number of irrelevant dimensions is the same in the two experiments.

and concept complexity but differ in terms of the elaborateness of concept-response associations which must be formed.

The results of the two studies are shown in Figure 4. In the Bulgarella-Archer study, as the number of relevant dimensions increased, trials, errors, and time to problem solution increased in a roughly linear fashion. Each added relevant dimension resulted in a constant increment in task difficulty. On the other hand, in the Walker-Bourne study, an increase in the number of relevant dimensions produced a disproportionate increase in task difficulty. Adding the third relevant dimension had a much more marked effect on difficulty than did adding the second. It is probable that the difference in response complexity between the two studies accounts for the discrepant results. In the Walker-Bourne experiment the change from two to three relevant dimensions not only (*a*) increased the number of stimulus attributes whose importance the subject must discover and use but also (*b*) produced an expansion of the response system from four to eight categories. Factor *a*, which is the only one operating in the Bulgarella-Archer results, probably adds some fixed amount to task difficulty. Factor *b*, which exerts its effect only in the Walker-Bourne results, contributes another increment in difficulty, making the outcome of the study different from that of Bulgarella and Archer.

It is well to note another procedural difference between the two experiments. Walker and Bourne constructed their stimulus materials from geometric forms and presented them visually to the subject. Bulgarella and Archer used auditory signals. Any comparison between these experiments, such as the one above, must then be qualified until we know more about how conceptual behavior is affected by the mode of stimulus information.

STIMULUS FACTORS

Stimulus materials in one form or another—objects, pictures, words, and so forth—afford the raw material from which concepts are derived. It should come as no surprise to find that characteristics of the stimuli, for example, their complexity, their discriminability, and their mode of presentation, have profound effects on conceptual behavior. Research on the problem has been stimulated and guided by Hovland's (1952) analysis of the informational content of the stimulus in conceptual problems. While Hovland was mainly concerned with the issue of how readily a human subject uses information about a concept which is available in positive and negative instances, the contribution of his analysis goes beyond this question. He provided both a technical definition of the stimulus and the basis for rigorous manipulations of stimulus variables which until then had been treated all too vaguely in experimentation.

Positive and Negative Instances

When the problem calls for the identification of a single concept, the stimuli presented to the subject are of two types: positive—those which illustrate the concept and therefore contain all its essential features; and negative—those which do not illustrate the concept. Smoke (1933) reported an experiment which seemed to show that negative instances conveyed very little if any information to the subject about the concept. Hovland (1952) showed that Smoke's results could in large measure be attributed to the facts that (a) subjects did not know the limits or dimensionality of the stimulus population to which the concept applied, (b) subjects did not know the type or nature of the concept to be identified, and (c) the amount of logical information about the concept was far less in negative than in positive instances. Hovland argued that, unless the subject is told about or assumes certain limits on the stimulus population, he may correctly consider a near infinitude of stimuli which exemplify what the concept is not (negative instances) while only a relative few illustrate what the concept is. Under these circumstances it is not surprising that negative instances convey little information.

Hovland pointed out that Smoke's work does not distinguish between two potential sources of difficulty in negative instances: (a) their low efficiency as carriers of logical information and (b) the subject's ability to assimilate information presented in this form. He suggested that one experimental approach to this distinction is to arrange concept problems with the amount of logical information conveyed by the two types of instances equated, and he developed a technique for constructing such problems.

Hovland and Weiss (1953) subsequently reported that, even with informational content equated, negative instances were more difficult to use for purposes of solving concept problems. More subjects completed their task successfully when all the instances were positive. Those presented with a mixture of positive and negative instances showed an intermediate level of performance. While these results are in line with Smoke's conclusion, it is clear from the Hovland-Weiss experiments that the difference is in large measure due to the subject's difficulty in using negative information about the concept. But, further, this study shows that, under proper conditions, negative instances are not valueless. A sizable proportion of subjects were able to identify concepts on the basis of negative instances only.

Freibergs and Tulving (1961) pointed out that the results of Hovland and Weiss may reflect transfer effects from preexperimental experience with concepts rather than some immutable difference in ability to use positive and negative information. It is more natural in everyday circumstances to encounter and to deal with positive instances, and rarely if ever are concepts formed or communicated by negative examples alone. If this is true, differences in the ability of naïve subjects to handle negative instances in a conceptual problem should vanish with compensating practice in the use of this type of information.

Freibergs and Tulving tested this hypothesis by giving subjects a series of 20 successive concept problems. The stimulus materials were geometric forms varying in three dimensions, each with four values. The problems were all conjunctive and each could be solved either by inspecting four positive or four negative instances. In each problem, half the subjects were shown the four necessary positive instances and were required to name the concept if they could. The remaining subjects were shown only the four necessary negative instances. Results of the study, plotted in time to reach solution, are shown in Figure 5. The experimenters set an arbitrary upper limit of 3.5

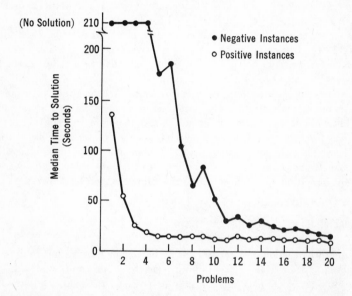

Figure 5. Median time to solution of 20 consecutive problems for subjects working with only positive or only negative instances. Data from Freibergs and Tulving (1961).

minutes for the subject to give his answer to each problem. (Note that no subject in the negative instance group solved the first 4 problems within that interval.) Despite this limit there is a clear difference between the groups on the initial tasks. After 11 or 12 practice problems, however, the group difference is drastically reduced, and at the end of the 20 problem series they are virtually the same.

These results both confirm and extend the Hovland-Weiss conclusion. Positive instances are used more efficiently than negatives by naïve subjects but not by those who have had some training. This finding is consistent with the hypothesis that the difference between instances is attributable to transfer effects from prior extralaboratory experience. A secondary result is the observation that performance improves with practice on both types of instances. This effect is reminiscent of learning set formation observed by Harlow in interproblem transfer experiments. It suggests that subjects acquire a rule or principle (in this case, conjunction) which transcends the relevant stimulus features of any single problem and can be applied to effect the correct combination of attributes in all problems of a given class.

Studies of positive and negative instances have been limited to concepts based on conjunctive and unidimensional rules. For an instance to be positive in these cases, it must contain all relevant attributes. According to Hovland's (1952) analysis, this fact means that in ordinary circumstances positive instances will carry more logical information about a concept than will negative instances. Further, it means that positive instances provide a natural focus for strategies which are useful in identifying relevant attributes (Bruner et al., 1956). But these advantages of positive over negative instances do not hold for concepts based on rules other than conjunction. For example, in disjunctive concepts—those based on the "and/or" rule—the informational value of positive and negative instances is reversed. Whereas positive instances contain one or more relevant attributes, negatives must embody no relevant attribute. Maximally efficient strategies should, therefore, focus on a negative instance. Concept identification should be easier with a series of all negative instances. These hypotheses have not yet been put to test experimentally, although Bruner et al. (1956) did report a preliminary study of disjunction concept formation aimed at detecting the strategies used by subjects.

Amount of Information

Another question brought to light by Hovland's analysis has to do with the absolute amount and type of information the subject must deal with in a conceptual problem. The question may be posed in the following way. The stimulus population in any problem is characterized by a set of dimensions, each of which takes on two or more values. All dimensions contribute some information to the stimulus situation. Some dimensions are relevant to problem solution in the sense that they define the concept(s) to be identified. Other dimensions are irrelevant and can be ignored. The number of relevant dimensions is directly related to the amount of relevant information (information necessarily used in problem solving). The number of irrelevant dimensions contributes similarly to the amount of irrelevant information. The subject's task is in part one of discovering which stimulus dimensions are relevant. Do the numbers of relevant and irrelevant dimensions, which determine the complexity of the stimulus population, affect problem difficulty?

There are several studies which provide evidence on the question, and the results are generally quite consistent. First, as the number of *irrelevant dimensions* increases, problem difficulty as measured by trials and errors to solution increases linearly (Bulgarella and Archer, 1962). Further, although there are no extensive studies to cite, the disrupting effect of irrelevant information occurs with the learning of temporal concepts or sequential regularities in stimuli as well as for the usual discrete geometric patterns (Bruner, Wallach, and Galanter, 1959; Barch, 1961). Second, as the number of *relevant dimensions* increases, so does problem difficulty, in either a linear (Bulgarella and Archer, 1962) or positively accelerated fashion (Walker and Bourne, 1961), depending on whether or not there is a corresponding increase in the complexity of the response system.

The above-mentioned studies have explored interdimensional stimulus variability; that is, stimulus complexity manipulated in terms of the number of different dimensions on which patterns vary. The complexity in a stimulus population is also a direct function of intradimensional variability; that is, the number of values each dimension is permitted to assume. Often, concept experiments use a minimal number of values, say, 2 or 3, on each dimension. What is the effect of increasing this number to 4 or 6 or 10? Clearly the number of different stimulus patterns will increase; thus the subject's problem should become more complicated because of heavier memory requirements among other possible factors.

The only experiment which has systematically explored intradimensional variability was reported by Battig and Bourne (1960). Stimulus material used took on 2, 4, or 6 values per dimension. Each problem had a two-dimensional conjunctive solution. With two-valued dimensions the subject was required to combine one value from each relevant dimension to effect a solution. With six-valued dimensions three values from both of the relevant dimensions, for example, three discriminably different shades of red and three different-shaped triangles, had to be combined. In the latter case, presumably, the subject had to use the more general concepts of redness and triangularity in solving the problem. Problem difficulty increased directly with number of values per dimension. This effect did not interact with or in any way change the basic relationship between performance and inter-dimensional variability which was manipulated as a second independent factor in the experiment. Performance got worse as the number of irrelevant dimensions increased, regardless of the amount of intradimensional variability. Although the issue of intradimensional variability is far from settled by this single study, the fact does remain that, in one case at least, this variable changes little but the over-all difficulty of a problem.

The Role of Redundant Stimulus Information

When we say that a stimulus population has a certain number of dimensions, for example, three—color, form, and size, each with a certain number of values; for example, two—red and green, square and triangle, large and small, we generally mean that the population consists of patterns showing all possible combinations of these characteristics. In the above example the population contains 2^3 or 8 different patterns, such as large red square, small red square, and so on. In general, the stimulus population will consist of V^D patterns, where D is the number of dimensions and V is the number of values. When one or more of the possible patterns is missing, some redundancy exists. Suppose all red patterns are large and all green patterns are small; the large greens and the small reds are missing. Here the size of a pattern is perfectly predictable from knowledge of its color (or vice versa). One does not need to see the size of a pattern if he knows its color, for in a certain sense size is completely determined by color. Thus, the information conveyed by (or contained in) these two dimensions is redundant.

Garner (1962) distinguished between two important characteristics of redundancy—its amount and its form. Amount of redundancy is defined in terms of the number of missing patterns or in terms of the number of overlapping dimensions; amount increases in proportion to the number of missing patterns. Form of redundancy is defined in terms of the particular patterns which are missing or dimensions which overlap. For example, if only the relevant dimensions overlapped, the form would be called "relevant stimulus redundancy."

Both amount and form of redundancy exert important effects on concept identification. Bourne and Haygood (1959, 1960, 1964) reported several experiments bearing on this conclusion. In one study two-category problems were constructed and presented with the reception paradigm. For different groups of subjects, the problem given had 1, 2, 3, 4, or 5 overlapping relevant dimensions. In the case of 3 redundant dimensions, for example, all large patterns were also red and square and were to be placed in one category, whereas all small patterns were green and triangular and were to be placed in the second category. Not only was it the case then that size, color, and form were mutually predictable but also one could categorize the patterns on the basis of any one (or some combination) of these dimensions. Problems had, in addition to the relevant features, 1, 3, or 5 irrelevant (and nonredundant) dimensions.

The results, as shown in Figure 6, indicated that, as relevant redundancy increased, performance improved. Apparently the provision of more bases on which a problem can be solved hastens the attainment of a solution. The facilitative effect was magnified in more complex problems—those with 3 and 5 irrelevant dimensions—but existed in significant strength even when no irrelevant dimensions were present.

In a second experiment, stimulus redundancy was introduced into the set of irrelevant dimensions. Problems were constructed with 2, 3, 4, and 5 redundant irrelevant dimensions such that the values on all were perfectly predictable from the knowledge of one dimension. Subjects solved problems with either a unidimensional or conjunctive (two nonredundant relevant dimensions) solution. As the number of irrelevant dimensions increased,

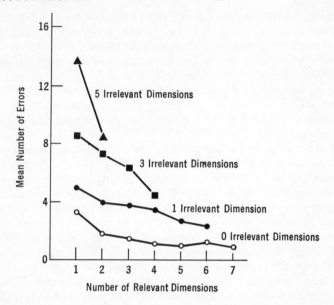

Figure 6. Mean number of errors made by subjects prior to solving the problem. Performance improves as number of redundant relevant dimensions increases and number of nonredundant irrelevant dimensions decreases. Data from Bourne and Haygood (1959, 1961).

performance got worse—and more so in the more complex conjunctive problems. However, the inhibiting effect of number of redundant irrelevant dimensions was less than the effect obtained in comparable conditions of nonredundant irrelevant dimensions. The difference is probably a result of the fact that redundant dimensions can be eliminated as a group to the extent that the subjects notice their covariation. But the deleterious effect obtained indicates that not all subjects did discover or utilize the redundancy in the set of irrelevant dimensions.

A comparison of these two studies shows that different effects can be expected from different forms of redundancy. Relevant redundancy facilitates and irrelevant redundancy interferes with performance. Both form and amount of redundancy are important determiners of performance in concept-identification problems.

Sensory Modality

Most natural concepts are defined by relevant attributes which affect several different sensory systems simultaneously. Members of the class of objects called "banana," for example, are yellow (visual), elongated (visual or tactual), soft (tactual), and rather sweet (taste and smell). While human beings are known to rely heavily on visual stimulation, it is common for them to combine information from various modalities in the formation and utilization of concepts. Whether or not the information coming from one sense modality is any more salient or obvious or any easier to assimilate in defining concepts is difficult to say. There are very few empirical studies of conceptual behavior which use other than visual stimuli; thus, there is a dearth of evidence on the relative value of visual and other types of information.

It is probably the case that shifting from the visual modality to some other, say, auditory or tactual, will have no major effect on the functional relationships between performance and important independent variables. The study by Bulgarella and Archer (1962), for example, suggests that the influence of number of irrelevant dimensions is the same for auditory and visual stimulus patterns. However, this experiment provides no real assurance of an invariance across modalities because it was not designed to compare directly visual and auditory information. For the same reason, it provided no assessment of the relative saliency of cues accessible to these modalities. There is only one study (Lordahl, 1961) in which the comparison between auditory and visual stimulus information has been made. Here subjects were required to sort patterns according to a conjunctive combination of one auditory and one visual attribute, for example, all stimulus patterns characterized by the simultaneous presentation of a circle and a high-pitched sound were positive instances. For different groups of subjects the stimulus patterns also varied on 0 through 4 irrelevant auditory dimensions and 0 through 4 irrelevant visual dimensions.

The results for amount of irrelevant visual information were consistent with earlier studies; as the number of dimensions increased, performance got worse linearly. Increasing the amount of irrelevant auditory information had *essentially* the same effect, though less in amount. The author concluded that subjects were less attentive to auditory signals (of the nonlinguistic variety used in this experiment) so that increases in their complexity had a less distracting influence. It is possible, then, to infer that relevant auditory attributes are more difficult to use, at least in conjunction with simultaneous visual stimulation, because of their lack of saliency. This hypothesis, however, remains to be tested directly.

Stimulus Sequence Effects

In an analysis of goal-oriented thinking, Underwood (1952) developed an important hypothesis concerning the interrelationships among stimulus events. This hypothesis involves the temporal contiguity of instances of the same concept and may be stated as follows: The closer together in time instances of a given concept occur, the more rapid will be the formation or identification of that concept. The hypothesis arises from an assumption that abstracting the properties relevant to a concept depends on the subject's ability to retain a sufficient number of contrasting positive instances. If stimulus instances are presented successively to the subject an increase in the time between instances may decrease the likelihood of complete retention, thus serving to retard concept learning. Still another factor could play an important role in the contiguity effect in certain experimental situations. If the subject is required to identify several concepts concurrently, the contiguity among instances of the same concept may be decreased by interpolating between them instances of one or more other concepts. By so doing, one would not only lengthen the time interval between instances of a given concept but also add a source of interference arising from the necessity to attend to, respond to, and remember instances of other concepts. Underwood's hypothesis can be restated for this case to imply important stimulus sequence effects in conceptual behavior. More specifically, performance should be considerably better, in multiple-concept problems, when all instances of a single concept are presented one after another without interpolation of instances of any other concept instead of when the instances of various concepts are scrambled or intermixed.

As a test of this hypothesis Kurtz and Hovland (1956) presented eight instances (geometric designs) of each of four concepts to subjects in either a mixed or an unmixed order. At the end of this series, subjects were asked to give a verbal description of each concept and to identify several test stimuli, each of which exemplified one of the four groupings. Following the unmixed order of presentation, subjects gave more correct test identifications and more correct verbal descriptions of concepts than following the mixed order. Newman (1956), using the conventional reception paradigm which required the subject to name a category for each successive stimulus, studied two mixed orders of presentation which differed in average number of inter- polated stimuli shown between instances of the same concept. The subjects learned nine concepts concurrently. The condition wherein instances of the same concept were closer together in the stimulus series led to significantly better over-all performance. The results of both experiments support Under- wood's hypothesis. They are somewhat limited, however, in the sense that only two conditions of stimulus contiguity were studied in each. In a subse- quent experiment Bourne and Jennings (1963) investigated four degrees of contiguity among the instances of four different concepts. They observed a linear improvement in performance, measured in total number of correct responses, with increased contiguity among the instances of each concept.

The most likely interpretation of these findings is based on memory interference resulting from the interpolation of instances of other concepts between examples of any one concept. A subject must retain sufficient informa- tion from positive instances of a concept to abstract their relevant or defining characteristics. In high contiguity cases, especially an unmixed series as used by Kurtz and Hovland, these memory requirements are minimized. There are obvious procedural differences among the three experiments discussed here. Both category responses and verbalized hypotheses were used as performance measures; from four to nine concurrent concepts were learned; and both subject-pacing and experimenter-pacing conditions were employed. Consistency in results over this range of variation indicates both the generality and theoretical power of Underwood's analysis.

An Order of Dominance or Abstractness Among Concepts

It seems clear that the concepts one deals with in everyday life differ in their abstractness. Some concepts, such as "barn," are relatively concrete and are based on perceptual or "thing-like" attributes. Others, such as "democracy," are more general and abstract, lacking easily perceptible features and/or empirical referents. We have noted earlier that the capacity for forming and dealing with abstract concepts seems to arise from language and the use of words symbolically to represent and to communicate ideas. Heidbreder (1945) performed some studies of conceptual abstractness suggested by her general theory of perceptual and cognitive processes. Put simply, the theory holds that the ease of forming a concept is a function of the degree to which its instances possess "thing-character." This notion rests on an assumption that human beings are innately capable of dealing more easily with concrete objects. While the theory is rather vague and informal by current standards, the research it generated has been useful.

In one study (Heidbreder, 1946) subjects were presented with 16 series of objects, each consisting of one instance of nine different concepts. Among the concepts to be learned were the following: three based on *concrete* objects, for example, "birds"; three based on *general* shape, for example, "circular"; and three based on *numerical* value. The ease with which each of these concept types was formed corresponded to the aforementioned hypothesis; that is, concrete objects were grouped most rapidly while numerical concepts were identified least rapidly. The result has been replicated by Heidbreder (1947), and similar findings have been reported by Grant (1951).

Thus it seems clear that differences, often referred to as an order of dominance, among these concept types do exist. There is little agreement with Heidbreder's original notions about the natural order of dominance among modes of human cognition, however. Osgood (1954) attributes the difficulty of abstract concepts to the relative unavailability of and/or the competition among mediating responses. The more concrete a concept is, the greater the probability that a single unambiguous label will already exist for it. Forms and numbers, on the other hand, are *aspects* of concrete objects; for example, a flower-shaped pattern could serve as an instance of the concept "circle." As such they tend to be more subject to interference from competing mediational responses when serving as the basis of a concept.

Later evidence suggests that some of the differences among Heidbreder's concept types may be a function of an uncontrolled variable in her experiments; namely, interstimulus similarity. Recall from Chapter III Gibson's (1940) emphasis on the role of stimulus similarity in verbal learning. Baum (1954) generalized Gibson's notions to concept learning and tested the hypothesis that, when several concepts are to be learned concurrently, those for which the instances are least discriminable from each other and most discriminable from instances of other concepts will be easiest to learn; conversely, concepts containing highly discriminable instances which bear some similarity to instances of other concepts will be most difficult to learn. Baum repeated one of Heidbreder's experiments using the same stimulus materials and gathering data on the discriminability (or confusability) of instances of all nine concepts. The concepts were attained essentially in the same order observed by Heidbreder. It was shown, however, that this order is inversely related to stimulus discriminability; that is, the more difficult concepts contained instances which tended to be more often confused with instances of other concepts. Thus, the results support a simpler and more rigorous basis for interpreting at least some significant portion of the abstractness effect in conceptual problems.

Concluding Remarks

In this section we have tried to provide a sampling of findings from research on stimulus conditions in conceptual behavior. A broad domain of variables has been explored. Consequently, summarization of the present state of knowledge is difficult. It might be said, however, that any manipulation of the stimulus which increases its complexity or informational load or which decreases the perceptibility of that information impedes the formation or identification of concepts based on it. Increasing the dimensionality of the stimulus population, spreading instances of a given concept out among instances of other concepts, presenting information in negative form, all have deleterious effects.

Theories of conceptual behavior, emphasizing basically different underlying processes, have done remarkably well in accounting for these effects. With respect to number of irrelevant stimulus dimensions, as an example, cue-conditioning theories point to the influence on the complexity of S-R associations, involving both relevant cues to be conditioned and (possibly) irrelevant cues to be adapted; hypothesis-testing models assign to the same variable an effect which increases the total number of initially plausible hypotheses, thus decreasing the probability of sampling the correct solution on any trial. These studies go a long way toward clearing up questions about certain facets of conceptual behavior. Further, they have provided a basis for continuing theoretical developments within both main lines discussed in Chapter III. They do not, however, weigh heavily on the side of any one theoretical position. The type of experiment which permits an infallible decision among theories is illusory and is not likely to be found among any of the present studies.

FACTORS OF INFORMATIVE FEEDBACK

In any learning problem, conceptual tasks included, two sources of information are available to the subject; namely, the stimulus and the informative feedback. We have seen how some characteristics of stimulus information serve to accelerate or to slow down concept formation. Variations in informative feedback—those signals which indicate something about the correctness of individual responses—have similar effects.

It is important to note that some researchers ascribe both informational and reinforcing value to feedback signals. That is, feedback has been interpreted as a source of reward (presumably when the subject is told his response is correct) and punishment (when the response is indicated to be wrong). While it is true that feedback signals play much the same role in human learning situations as do food pellets or shocks for a lower animal, there is some question about their incentive value. We shall explore a few cases wherein manipulations of informative feedback seem to have quite different effects than counterpart variations in reinforcement. The issue of a distinction between the reinforcing and informational value of any signal in a learning task is a difficult one to resolve, as some of the following research evidence will demonstrate.

Completeness of Informative Feedback

A potentially important aspect of feedback is the amount of information each signal provides about its associated response and about problem solution. Only a few experiments have sought to explore this question. In one study Bourne and Pendleton (1958) compared two conditions of feedback completeness in concept identification problems which required subjects to sort geometric patterns into four conjunctive categories. In one condition the subject was told on each trial whether his response was correct or incorrect. In the other condition the subject was, in addition, shown the correct response whenever he made an error. These two degrees of completeness were combined with three levels of task complexity, that is, problems with 1, 3, and 5 irrelevant dimensions, to gain more general evidence on possible performance differences. The results are summarized in Figure 7; feedback completeness was an effective variable with the correct-incorrect condition being significantly inferior to the condition wherein the correct response was indicated on every trial. Furthermore, as can be seen, the difference between these conditions was remarkably constant over the three levels of task complexity.

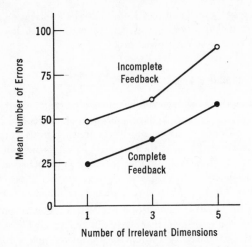

Figure 7. Mean number of errors to problem solution in conditions with complete (correct response category signalled on each trial) and incomplete (correct category not indicated on error-trials) feedback at three levels of task complexity. Data from Bourne and Pendleton (1958).

A related series of experiments has been undertaken by Buss and associates (for example, Buss and Buss, 1956). These researchers used basically the correct-incorrect feedback arrangement described above. However, for some subjects, feedback signals were provided only after correct responses (called the "right-nothing," or R-N case); for others, feedback was given only after incorrect responses (the "nothing-wrong," or N-W case). As a control still other subjects were given feedback on all trials (the R-W case). One may imagine that the R-W condition will yield significantly better performance than either R-N or N-W because of the greater completeness of information provided for the subject. The typical result, however, is that R-W and N-W are both superior to R-N and do not differ from each other. The proper interpretation of this finding is not clear. Buss ascribes the effect to a supposed greater "reinforcing" value for W signals relative to R. However, it is equally plausible to argue that the effect is due either to (a) the more frequent occurrence of W in the trial sequence—which results from the use of four-response problems wherein the probability of an error is three times as great as the probability of a correct response—or (b) the lesser ambiguity of W signals—an error signal tells the subject he is definitely on the wrong track, for if he "had the concept" no errors would be made; on the other hand, a correct response (followed by an R signal) can occur by chance even if the subject has not solved the problem.

These findings are in need of further elucidation. It is important to know, for example, what differences might obtain if R and W signals were equated in frequency across these conditions. But, while the information is spare, we have once again an indication of the importance of feedback completeness to efficient performance in conceptual tasks.

Probability of Informative Feedback

A variation on the foregoing experiments is the case in which informative feedback is omitted on some trials irrespective of the correctness of the subject's response. Does the subject merely ignore such trials so that solution is delayed in direct proportion to their frequency? Can something about the solution be learned on these trials, so that there is no commensurate reduction in over-all performance? Or do these trials have an inhibiting effect which makes for disproportionate interference with the attainment of concepts?

The correct alternative seems to be the last, at least in the results of Bourne and Pendleton (1958). In that study different groups of subjects were required to solve four-category conjunctive problems under conditions in which feedback was omitted on 0%, 10%, 20%, or 30% of trials. The increment in trials to solution was greater than the number of trials without feedback. This result is probably attributable to certain memory factors. It is clear that solving problems depends on remembering several instances of the same concept in order to abstract their common features. When feedback is omitted, the subject does not learn which of several concepts the given instance exemplifies. This means that between instances of the same concept a number of "neutral" stimuli will occur in proportion to feedback probability and will act as distractors or sources of interference (just as interpolated instances of other concepts, for example, Kurtz and Hovland, 1956). These added stimuli exert a predictable inhibiting effect on over-all performance in the problem.

Confirming Feedback for an Irrelevant Dimension

Part of the difficulty one has in locating and identifying the relevant attributes of a concept may be a result of ambiguity in informative feedback signals. On any given trial, feedback may confirm some hypotheses based on irrelevant attributes (or reinforce irrelevant dimensions); it is only over a series of trials that a subject can discover the inconsistency of irrelevant attributes. Usually, feedback which confirms or reinforces an irrelevant attribute occurs with chance probability in conceptual problems. For example, if redness is an irrelevant attribute from a binary dimension (red versus green) one would expect it to be associated with the positive response on 50% of trials. If one were to increase the frequency with which redness is associated with the positive category (and, correspondingly, increase the frequency of green in the negative category) it is reasonable to expect some interference with the process of identifying the true relevant attribute(s). In this case we would increase the ambiguity of the irrelevant color dimension by increasing its confirming feedback (or rate of reinforcement).

Gormezano and Grant (1958) undertook such a study and obtained the expected results. As the degree of association between the levels of an irrelevant dimension and the conceptual categories increased from 0% through 75% of trials, discovery of the relevant dimension was delayed. When a nonreversal shift in solution to the formerly irrelevant dimension was introduced degree of prior partial reinforcement for that dimension had no effect on performance. Subjects learned of the relevance of the new dimension in the same number of trials regardless of whether that dimension was never reinforced (0%) or frequently reinforced (75%) in the first problem. This the authors interpreted as running counter to a simple S-R reinforcement theory which would predict that the greater the prior association between the dimension and the response categories the faster eventual learning should be. Gormezano and Grant indicated, however, that their data could be accounted for with an S-R reinforcement theory amplified by mediational mechanisms which permit the subject to maintain an orientation only to the truly relevant dimension in the first problem and not at all to the intermittently reinforced irrelevant dimension.

Probabilistic Concepts

In the vast majority of problems given in experiments, the concepts to be learned are deterministic. Each instance either does or does not illustrate the concept. The relevant attributes of an instance, once known, allow one to infer with certainty the class or category to which it belongs. Bruner *et al.* (1956; see also Brunswik, 1952) point out that in real life we are often forced to deal with probabilistic concepts; that is, categories which cannot be predicted with certainty from knowledge of the relevant attributes. In these cases there are no fully valid cues in any single instance to the category or response to be associated with that instance. Thus, there arise some empirical and theoretical questions about the ease with which probabilistic concepts are learned, the strategies which subjects may use in attaining them, and the manner in which they are used once the relevant attributes have been identified.

Goodnow and Postman (1955), Pishkin (1960), and Bruner *et al.* (1956) all reported experiments on the attainment of probabilistic concepts. In the procedures of these studies, concept uncertainty was introduced by presenting misinformative or misleading feedback signals on a certain percentage of trials. To illustrate, suppose the concept to be identified is "redness." Ordinarily, whenever a red object is presented the positive category would be signalled after the subject makes his response. Likewise, the negative category would be indicated for all nonred patterns. To produce a probabilistic category, feedback was used sometimes to indicate to the subject that he had responded correctly (or incorrectly) when in fact the reverse was true. That is, on some trials a red pattern would be indicated as belonging in the negative category (or a green one in the positive category). It is, of course, this use of informative feedback in the definition of probabilistic concept which leads us to discuss the issue here rather than in some other section.

The results of these studies were quite consistent. Subjects were able to identify the relevant attributes, even with 40% misinformative trials. But rather than categorizing all patterns containing the (partially valid) relevant attributes in the same category, subjects engaged in a certain amount of "guessing behavior." To return to our example, in the later learning trials subjects were observed to respond with the negative category to red patterns (and the positive category to green ones) on a percentage of trials roughly equivalent to the percentage of misinformative signals. In other words, in an apparent attempt to outguess the experimenter, subjects matched the probability structure of the stimulus-response assignments. This is not a particularly rational approach to solving the problem, for it leads to fewer correct responses than does the principle of always responding positively to the relevant attribute.

Some subjects in the above-mentioned studies *did* adopt a rational strategy rather than probability matching. Thus, probability matching may be a transitory stage in performance which yields subsequently to the more consistent approach. All these studies allowed subjects relatively few trials in which to learn. It is plausible that probability matching tendencies would vanish with longer practice. Indirect evidence on an initial temporary tendency to match the probability with which response alternatives occur even with deterministic concepts is provided by Mandler, Gold, and Cowan (1963). To test this hypothesis with probabilistic concepts, Bourne (1963a) undertook an experiment similar to Pishkin's wherein the subjects were given 600 trials of practice involving 10%, 20% and 30% of misinformative feedback. The results showed that 42 of 60 subjects eventually learned to respond consistently on the basis of the partially valid, relevant attribute. Most of these subjects were shown to pass through an intermediate stage of probability matching before attaining the more rational solution. Furthermore, all subjects were able to transfer this mode of responding to a second problem with different attributes and a different percentage of misinformation.

In summary, the results of these studies indicate that subjects can identify partially valid stimulus attributes and learn the structure of probabilistic concepts, although the process is slower than for deterministic categories. Moreover, while people at first use these attributes and concepts probabilistically, sufficient experience with specific examples leads to a more rational use; that is, one which maximizes the chances of making a correct response. Finally, as with pure, deterministic concept learning, transfer from one probabilistic concept to another is generally positive.

Remark

Like the stimulus, feedback provides the learner with an external source of information useful in guiding individual responses and in delimiting problem solution. The stimulus provides a cue or cues to the proper response on any trial; feedback contains information relevant to the way the subject should respond on future trials. The subject must combine these two sources of information to effect a solution to any problem. It would be anticipated then that manipulations of the informational content of feedback will have important effects on performances—just as the analogous variations in stimulus features do. By and large, these expectations are borne out by research. Any reduction in the completeness, probability, veridicality, and so on of informative feedback results in an impediment to problem solving.

TEMPORAL FACTORS

A certain amount of time is required to scan and to assimilate information in a complex stimulus display. Overt responses to comprehensible stimuli occur with some delay and only after a determinable execution time. Memorizing or making inferences from available data are time-consuming activities. Given an interval after learning during which interfering events may operate, some forgetting will probably occur. Even when solution to some problem is said to happen in a moment of insight, it is unsafe to assume that time spent in preparation, incubation, or in the "process of insight" itself is negligible. Perception, learning, inference, memory, discovery, and other activities bound up in conceptual behavior have measurable temporal characteristics. To the extent that environmental conditions limit or otherwise affect these characteristics, we may expect corresponding changes in the nature of a person's performance.

We noted earlier the emphasis Underwood (1952) put on time as a variable in general goal-oriented thinking. Underwood was concerned primarily with the temporal contiguity of instances of some concept to be learned; we discussed a few experiments which tested and supported his predictions. We proceed now to discuss several studies of different, but no less significant, temporal variables affecting performance.

Delay of Informative Feedback

One potentially important interval in conceptual tasks is the time between a subject's response on any trial and the presentation of feedback. Suppose that immediately after a subject responds the stimulus pattern is removed (see Figure 2) and he must wait some prescribed period of time before learning whether or not his answer was correct. Any delaying of feedback could plausibly lessen the informational content of the stimulus, for it forces the subject to rely on memory to bridge the time gap between stimulus and feedback and to make effective use of the information.

While many studies have shown a detrimental effect of delayed reward or reinforcement on performance by lower animals in simple learning situations, there are actually very few experiments with human subjects. Bourne (1957) reported one such experiment, using the reception paradigm, which enforced 0, .5, 1, 2, 4, and 8 second delays between response and feedback for different groups of subjects. The subjects were required to identify four concepts concurrently, based on the combinations of levels within two relevant dimensions. The results of the study were straightforward. As delay increased, performance got worse, with the inhibiting effect of delay increasing in magnitude with task complexity.

Several subsequent studies of delayed feedback in different but equally complex human-learning tasks failed to show any deleterious effect, however. There arises then a question about the replicability of data. Furthermore, a careful inspection of the procedural details of Bourne's experiment reveals that another variable—the time interval separating informative feedback and the presentation of the next stimulus, that is, the postfeedback interval—was confounded with delay of informative feedback. In order to maintain a constant interstimulus interval in all problems, postfeedback time was decreased to compensate for increases in delay. It is not unreasonable to expect an effect on performance due to length of postfeedback interval, for this interval affords the subject time to assimilate, "think over," and draw inferences from both the stimulus and the feedback signal of the trial. Moreover, this effect, if important, would result in performance trends similar to those observed by Bourne because, as noted, the postfeedback interval decreased as delay of feedback increased.

Variations in the Postfeedback Interval

The only way to learn which of two variables is really the important determiner of performance is to study them independently. Thus, in order to clarify the problem of time intervals, an experiment was required which embodied several different delay of feedback conditions, all with a constant postfeedback interval, and several different postfeedback lengths, all with a constant delay. Such an investigation was executed by Bourne and Bunderson (1963). The experimental plan involved nine basic conditions which were formed by combining three delay intervals, 0, 4, and 8 seconds, with three postfeedback intervals, 1, 5, and 9 seconds. These particular intervals were chosen because they produce three temporal arrangements identical to those in the earlier study of delay, namely, 0-9, 4-5, and 8-1, where the first digit refers to delay and the second to length of postfeedback interval. This experimental plan was replicated, once with simple problems involving two relevant and one irrelevant dimension and again with more complex problems using two relevant and five irrelevant dimensions.

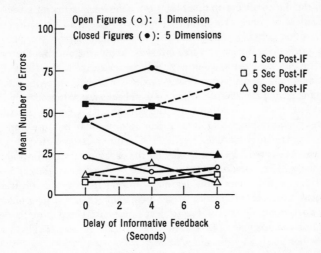

Figure 8. Mean number of errors to solution as a function of length of delay of informative feedback and length of the postfeedback interval. Two levels of task complexity are represented. Results show a minimal effect of delay and a strong effect of postfeedback interval length, especially in problems with five irrelevant dimensions. The dashed lines connect conditions common to this and an earlier study of delayed feedback reported by Bourne (1957). The results suggest that the previously observed inhibiting effect of delay was an artifact of failing to control length of the postfeedback interval. Data from Bourne and Bunderson (1963).

The results are best described graphically. In Figure 8 it can be seen that delay of informative feedback exerts no systematic effect on performance over the range of values used. There is, however, a marked improvement in performance as the postfeedback interval increases in duration. Moreover, the effect is greater in the more complex problems. Also shown in Figure 8 are the trends observed in the preceding study of delayed feedback. The effect of delay apparent in that study is shown to be an artifact of a failure to control the postfeedback interval.

While it had no significant effect on performance in this experiment, it would be unrealistic to conclude that feedback delay is generally ineffective. The intervals used were short, no greater than 8 seconds, and were filled with no interpolated activity. One might reasonably expect that, with longer delay intervals and/or intervals wherein the subject engaged in other activities (a condition which more nearly parallels the delay of reinforcement studies with lower animals), significant retarding influences would be recorded.

The results of the study suggest that learning does not take place immediately and automatically as a function of informative feedback (reinforcement) as some theories might seem to suggest. If this were the case, length of postfeedback interval should have no unique effect on performance.

Rather, the data indicate that subjects used the interval to rehearse, memorize, or otherwise process the information they had been given by the stimulus
and its accompanying feedback. Obviously, some kind of task-relevant
activity takes place during this free interval. As Bourne and Bunderson point
out, one might assert in keeping with S-R associational theory that the cue-
conditioning (and adapting) processes continue into the postfeedback interval
thereby increasing the amount of learning on each trial. Alternatively, it may
be argued that the interval provides the opportunity for a subject to revise
his current hypothesis in the light of new information. Because hypothesis-
testing theories (for example, Restle, 1962) often assume that a working
hypothesis is rejected (or revised) only on the occasion of an error (only when
it leads the subject to make an incorrect category response) while conditioning
theories assert that important learning processes occur on all trials, an
experiment in which the length of the postfeedback interval is made contingent on the correctness of the subject's response could provide decisive
evidence on the adequacy of these two theoretical positions. Such an experiment has not yet been reported.

Obviously, the facilitative effect which results from lengthening the
postfeedback interval must diminish at some point. Indeed, excessively long
intervals could have a retarding influence if they allowed for a significant
amount of forgetting from one trial to the next. To explore the problem,
Bourne, Guy, Dodd, and Justesen (1965) conducted an experiment which
contained intervals ranging from 1 through 25 seconds. They observed the
same facilitating effect up to an optimal interval, beyond which performance
got slightly worse. The optimum for simple problems (one irrelevant dimension) was shorter, around 9 seconds, than that for more complex tasks (five
irrelevant dimensions), about 17 seconds, which suggests that more time is
required to "think about" or assimilate the information given when, in fact,
that information (number of variable stimulus dimensions) is greater in
amount.

Distribution of Practice

Distribution of practice is defined by the spacing of practice trials in
time or by the degree of interpolated rest among work periods. In a sense
the length of postfeedback interval and perhaps also delay of feedback may
be thought of as conditions of practice distribution. It is clear from the
foregoing research that where and when rest is permitted makes some difference in the performance effects that result.

When the term "distribution of practice" has been used explicitly in
studies of concept learning (for example, Oseas and Underwood, 1952; Brown
and Archer, 1956) it has referred to the introduction of periodic rests between
blocks of trials of arbitrary length. In the Oseas and Underwood study, rest
intervals of length 6, 15, 30, and 60 seconds were provided, for independent

groups of subjects working on the same conceptual problem, after each block of nine stimuli. Every stimulus in a block was a positive instance of one of nine concepts learned concurrently. In the Brown-Archer experiment, rests of 0, 30, or 60 seconds were introduced after each block of 16 trials, which included four instances of each of four concepts. Task difficulty was independently varied in the later study in order to gain more general information on the possible effects of rest intervals.

The results of the two experiments are quite similar. <u>Periodic rests have at best only a slight facilitative effect on over-all performance.</u> In the Oseas and Underwood data, 15, 30, and 60 second groups all performed better than the 6 second group but did not differ among themselves. In the Brown and Archer study there was no reliable difference among rest conditions although longer intervals did result in superior performance on practice trials late in the learning process. One might wonder why it is that an intratrial interval (postfeedback) can have such a marked effect in concept learning while intertrial intervals are of minor benefit at best. The question has no easy answer. However, consider that each trial in a conceptual problem provides some unique information toward solution. This information may supply the basis of associating new relevant cues to the correct response category (or adapting irrelevant cues) or for revising a not-quite-adequate hypothesis. A "time-out" interval given on each trial allows these supposed processes to run their course. A time-out given only after every nth trial permits the subject to utilize whatever information he can retain from the preceding sequence. Knowing what we do about human memory (for example, Kurtz and Hovland, 1956) under these circumstances, however, retained information may well be limited to one or two trials at best. If this is so the outcome of the above-mentioned experiments is not surprising. The argument implies a testable hypothesis. The length of trial block or the number of stimuli responded to between each rest should be a significant variable determining the amount of facilitation resulting from rest. The fewer trials between each rest (keeping total rest-time constant), the greater the effect to be expected. An experiment designed to test this deduction may very well serve to clarify some of the ambiguity in our present knowledge of timing variables in conceptual behavior.

TYPES OF CONCEPTS—CONCEPTUAL RULES

In Chapter II we pointed out that any concept is describable in terms of a set of relevant attributes and a rule which combines or prescribes the function of or relationship among these attributes. The vast majority of studies of conceptual behavior have been concerned with conditions which affect the learning or identification of relevant attributes rather than with the learning or use of rules. Until now we have been talking almost exclusively about attribute identification. Furthermore, we shall be concerned largely with research on this kind of problem in the chapter which follows. The fact of the matter is that very little is known about rule learning and rule utilization. Only a few experiments related to these behavioral processes have been undertaken. Attribute identification experiments have typically minimized the importance of the rule-component of concepts by (*a*) basing the problem on simple and familiar rules such as conjunction or affirmation and (*b*) providing thorough preliminary instructions and training to the subject about the rule to be used. Problems wherein the rule is an element to be learned or discovered have simply not been studied very often.

There are a few experiments, however, which provide information on rule learning. This section is essentially a digression from the main stream of discussion so that we may review these experiments. Because they provide interesting and important leads toward an understanding of human conceptual behavior it is safe to say that many more intensive investigations along these lines will be undertaken in the future.

Differences Among Rules in Difficulty

There is suggestive evidence in the work of Bruner *et al.* (1956) that disjunctive concepts are more difficult to learn or identify than conjunctive, although a direct comparison of the two types was not made. The first systematic investigation of possible differences in rule difficulty was reported by Hunt and Hovland (1960). These researchers studied which of three different rules a subject would choose if all were consistent with a particular grouping of stimuli. Two of the rules, conjunction ("and") and disjunction ("and/or"), have already been described. The third, called the "relational rule," specifies a certain relationship, such as "greater than" or "equal to," between specific stimulus attributes. As an example one relational concept used by these experimenters was, "Same number of figures in the upper and lower portions of a stimulus card." The subject was presented with a series of geometric designs, some of which were labeled as positive instances, some of which were labeled as negative. The instances were selected in such a way that the positive class could be described logically either as a conjunctive, a disjunctive, or a relational concept. Which concept, if any, the subject discovered while inspecting these stimuli was determined in a subsequent series of test trials. In the test the subject was required to pick out the stimuli which he thought were consistent with (were positive instances of) the concept illustrated by the original stimulus series. Conjunctive and relational concepts were chosen with greater frequency than disjunctive concepts but did not differ from each other.

One may interpret frequency of choice as an indication of the relative difficulty of each rule or type of solution. If so, we would conclude on the basis of the Hunt and Hovland data that relational and conjunctive concepts are easier than disjunctives. This finding raises a number of additional questions. As examples we might ask: (1) Will the same result hold if we look at the learning process directly rather than require the subject to recognize positive instances after learning presumably has been completed? (2) If the result does hold up under various procedural conditions, what are the significant contributory factors? (3) Given that differences in difficulty among rules do exist, are they in any way affected by practice?

Conant and Trabasso (1964) and Neisser and Weene (1962) reported evidence related to the first two of these questions. In the Conant-Trabasso experiment, subjects were required to discover the solution to structurally equivalent conjunctive and disjunctive problems under a selection paradigm. All subjects solved problems of both types, presented in counterbalanced order. Consistent with the conclusion of Hunt and Hovland, disjunctive concepts were reliably more difficult to solve than conjunctive. These researchers were able further to trace at least part of the difference between rules to the relative difficulty of negative and positive instances. In terms of logical information, negative instances are more valuable than positive when the solution is a disjunction, while just the reverse is true for conjunctive problems. Conant and Trabasso showed that subjects learned more readily to use the information available in positive instances, thus putting them at somewhat of a disadvantage in disjunctive problems. From the earlier results of Freibergs and Tulving (1961), however, we would expect the differences between conjunctive and disjunctive problems to lessen or disappear with extensive practice in the use of negative information. One additional finding in this experiment was that subjects' card selections were more redundant (provided overlapping information) in disjunctive problems. This also may be due to the difficulty subjects have in understanding the full implications of a negative instance. Because the information they contain is difficult to assimilate and utilize, several stimuli providing essentially the same information may be required by the subject.

The study reported by Neisser and Weene (1962) is distinguished by its use of a large variety of different rules for forming concepts. These experimenters showed that there are ten different rules for generating nominal concepts based on (at most) two relevant attributes. Further, they indicated that these rules fall into three structurally different levels of complexity. On Level I are two rules: affirmation—all stimuli with attribute x are members of the concept; and negation—all stimuli which do not display attribute x are members of the concept. On the next higher level (II) are a set of rules which specify either a conjunctive or disjunctive combination of two attributes; for example, x and y or not x and/or y. Finally, on Level III are combinations of two attributes which involve both conjunctive and disjunctive rules; for example, (x and y) and/or (not x and not y). Successive levels represent increasing conceptual (or rule) complexity both in terms of the length of expression and in terms of hierarchical structure. Concepts at each level are composed of concepts from the next lower level. Neisser and Weene explored the learning of concepts at each level on the assumption that problem difficulty would increase with the structural complexity of a concept.

Significant changes in difficulty were observed as the level of concept increased. The outcome was interpreted as reflecting a hierarchical organization of conceptual processes within the subject. To attain a complex concept, the subject must use, and therefore must have attained earlier, some simpler concepts from lower levels. Complex learning and problem solving is predicated on earlier and simpler learning processes. While one may question this interpretation on several grounds (there is no real evidence that the subjects did learn Level III concepts as a combination of conjunctions and disjunctions), the fact still remains that rule differences do exist in significant degree, indicating again the real function of the rule as an item of knowledge to be discovered and used in any conceptual task.

Rule Learning

While Neisser and Weene point to structural complexity as a factor determining the difficulty of any concept, Bruner *et al.* (1956), Hunt and Hovland (1960), and others have suggested that natural experience with concepts in every day living may also be a major factor. The notion is that for one reason or another conjunctive and relational combinations of attributes are much more frequent and familiar than are disjunctive groupings or any other type. This argument would imply that a person can, with sufficient practice, learn to form or to identify disjunctive concepts just as readily as conjunctions. Wells (1963) explored this possibility in an experiment patterned after that of Hunt and Hovland. Subjects were first shown an array of positive and negative instances which could be described either as conjunctive or disjunctive concepts and were asked to name the concept. Nearly all subjects reported the conjunctive rule. Two subgroups of subjects were then given either two or four additional problems by a similar procedure but in which only a disjunctive solution was correct. Control subjects were given the same amount of training on problems which, like the first, could be solved either as a conjunction or disjunction. After training, all subjects were given a final test problem which could be solved by either rule. On the test those groups given training with disjunctive problems showed a significantly greater tendency than controls to identify the disjunctive solution. Thus, Wells argues, previous (preexperimental) experiences with natural concepts probably produced an initial favoritism for conjunctive solutions but that this preference can be overcome, at least in part, by moderate degrees of training.

Comment

We have noted that any specific concept may be defined in terms of a set of relevant stimulus attributes and a rule for combining them. In all the foregoing studies comparing different rules, except the Conant-Trabasso experiment, both the rule and the relevant attributes were unknown to the subject at the outset. In order to solve a problem, the subject in a sense had to discover both unknowns. Differences in the difficulty of such problems could result from either or both of two sources: (a) Some rules may be intrinsically harder to learn or to use in combining attributes; or (b) it is more difficult to identify the relevant attributes under certain rules as compared to others. If neither the rule nor the attributes are known to a subject when he begins a problem, it is impossible to separate these two potential sources of difficulty and to assess their independent effects.

The natural analytic approach to an investigation of these factors is to design experimental tasks wherein one of the problem aspects, either rule or relevant attributes, is known to the subject while the other must be learned or discovered from information presented in the form of positive and negative instances. Comparison of attribute identification tasks based on different but known (to the subject) rules would provide evidence on the possibility that relevant attributes are more difficult to discover under certain rules as compared to others. Conversely, a comparison of rule learning or rule identification tasks, wherein the relevant attributes are given to the subject at the outset, would indicate whether rule difficulty is independent of the necessity to identify attributes. Conant and Trabasso (1963) actually did use attribute identification problems in their study of rule difficulty; both the conjunctive and disjunctive rules were described to subjects before the problem was given. From the results of this experiment it may be concluded that the process of identifying relevant attributes will differ with the rule; disjunctive problems were significantly more difficult to solve. There is, however, the possibility that instructions in this experiment were not sufficient to communicate a full understanding of the disjunctive rule to all subjects.

More on Rule Difficulty

Haygood and Bourne (1965) compared the performance of human subjects on four different rules, *conjunction*, *disjunction*, *joint denial* (only patterns which are *neither A nor B* are positive instances of the concept, where A and B are the relevant attributes), and *conditional* (*if* a pattern contains *A then* it must also contain *B* to be a positive instance), and under three different conditions—attribute identification, rule learning, and complete learning. All subjects were given a series of five successive problems of the same type so that practice and transfer effects could be observed. For subjects working in the attribute identification condition the required rule was explained and illustrated prior to the first problem and then described again between each successive problem thereafter. In the rule-learning condition the two relevant attributes were named prior to each problem. Neither the rule nor the attributes were specified in complete learning. For any subject the same rule held for all five problems, though the relevant attributes changed from problem to problem. The reception paradigm was used throughout.

Rules differed markedly in difficulty on Problem 1 with conditional and disjunctive rules producing the greatest numbers of errors and trials to solution. However, these differences gradually diminished with successive problems, indicating that at least part of the differences among rules may be a function of their relative familiarity. In general, performance was worst in complete-learning conditions and best in rule-learning conditions. Performance approached perfection over five rule-learning problems; that is, subjects made almost no errors on the fifth problem for three of the rules. Performance levels in attribute identification and complete learning conditions were nearly the same after five problems. The latter finding suggests that subjects did learn the rules in the course of training and that remaining differences among the rules were due to the difficulties each presents for identifying relevant attributes. It seems clear from this experiment that differences in rule difficulty arise from both sources discussed earlier. First, rules differ in and of themselves probably because subjects are more experienced with some (for example, conjunctive) than with others (for example, disjunctive). Second, rules differ because it is analytically or strategically easier to identify the relevant attributes for some. Whether both sources of rule differences can be completely overcome with sufficient practice and experience remains to be demonstrated.

Other Rules

A concept is usually understood to be a grouping of things or perhaps more correctly a partition of things into positive and negative classes. As such, a concept is a nominal and discrete system of classification. Practically all experimental studies of conceptual behavior, including those reviewed in this section, have employed tasks based on rules which produce nominal classifications. Most of these rules are formally equivalent to or derivable from the basic operators of logic—for example, conjunction, disjunction, and negation.

Adams (1953) has suggested a more liberal definition of a concept which would include ordered, quantitative relationships between stimulus attributes and response categories. This viewpoint considers the traditional nominal task to be just one level of concept. On a different level are mathematical or functional expressions which prescribe some numerical response, given a set of numerical stimulus values. As an example, if A and B are two relevant stimulus dimensions which may take on a large number of values, a_i and b_j, and R_{ij} is the response, $R_{ij} = a_i + b_j$ is a concept. More complex examples, such as $R_{ij} = a_i \cdot b_j$ or $R_{ij} = .5a_i + .5b_j{}^2$, are, of course, possible. As in the nominal case, these concepts are analyzable into rules and attributes, the rules being such familiar operations as addition, multiplication, and the like. Problems such as these are quite well known, although they may not always be thought of as conceptual. Rigorous investigation of the conditions affecting the efficiency of learning mathematical functions and their utilization in solving problems has great practical as well as theoretical importance. Although there has been little laboratory work on these problems, recent evidence of interest (Uhl, 1963) suggests that we can expect considerably more research in the future.

CONCLUDING COMMENT

In the last 15 years psychologists have produced an impressive amount of research pertaining to the effects of task variables on performance in conceptual problems. Characteristics of the stimuli, responses, informative feedback and timing, and the nature of the conceptual rule all act to determine the speed and efficiency with which solutions are attained. It is probably fair to say that the bulk of research has centered around variables of the task, largely because they are open to relatively easy objective manipulation. The stability and reliability of functional relationships between task variables and performance is a result in part of their direct access to manipulation, control, and measurement. But, of course, task factors are not the only ones that influence behavior in problematic situations. The organism brings an indeterminate number of conditions with him to the task. His intelligence, memory, perceptual abilities, and so on have probable relevance to how well he will perform, regardless of the external conditions imposed. These variables, however, are not easy to manipulate, control, and measure. Thus, a researcher may tend to shy away from them or to balance them out of his experiments by one or another procedural device. Those intrepid souls who undertake to study organismic variables often find horrendous data variability resulting from crude, inefficient investigative techniques. Despite the ponderous difficulties some headway toward a real understanding of these variables is being made, and although conclusions may be tentative and highly qualified, a body of useful information is being collected. It is to this topical area that we turn in the next chapter.

V

Conditions of the
Performing Subject

THE PRESENT DISCUSSION CENTERS on relations between characteristics of the problem solver and his performance in a conceptual task. It is organized, like the last chapter, into sections each of which reviews the study of a particular broadly defined variable.

Reflecting the technical difficulties of research on subject variables is a lack of sustained, programmatic experimentation. Often the available data are fragmentary and compel few strong conclusions. As a result, we shall make no effort at an exhaustive account, but rather we shall purposefully limit the discussion to those conditions and processes on which the research is sufficient to yield a reasonable amount of clear and useful information.

MEMORY

In experiments using the reception paradigm, a subject is shown a series of stimulus patterns from some well-defined population. When the instances are presented successively so that only one is available for inspection at any given time, the principal task of inducing a concept to fit the positive and negative classes is complicated by the necessity to remember information over several trials. This follows from the fact that no single instance contains sufficient information to specify the concept. The same complication arises in the selection paradigm if the subject must remember which of the previously chosen stimuli were positive and which were negative instances. The fallibility of human memory may account in some part for the common finding that subjects generally need to be presented with more instances than are logically necessary to determine the concept.

While there are, no doubt, individual differences in ability to retain information, there appear to be no studies of the extent to which this variability is related to performance on conceptual problems. There are, however, several ways to manipulate environmental conditions so as to affect the extent to which memory is required by the task. Studies exploring those conditions provide important information on the role that memory plays in conceptual behavior.

Doing Problems "in the Head"

One simple memory experiment was conducted by Bruner, Goodnow, and Austin (1956). In it each subject was given two successive conjunctive problems to solve under the usual selection paradigm with the entire stimulus population in full view. On a final problem the stimulus array was removed and the subject was forced to solve the problem "in his head." In other words, on the last problem the subject had to rely completely on memory for the stimulus population and of the successive stimuli he selected. Performance was much worse on the last problem as compared to the first two, even though practice effects should have facilitated its solution. More important, however, were the effects this added memory requirement had on the subject's strategy. First of all, stimulus selections tended to be much more redundant in the third problem. Subjects would often select two or more stimuli which supplied essentially the same information about the relevancy of attributes. Second, selections were much less systematic, often reflecting a failure on the part of subjects to recall previously tested and rejected hypotheses. More than half the subjects used some form of focusing on the first two problems. These subjects did relatively well on the last problem compared to those who adopted a scanning approach. Scanning, as we noted, imposes heavy memory requirements itself so that when these subjects were forced to work a problem in their heads performance became quite inefficient. Scanners required almost three times as many stimulus selections as focusers on the last problem. Thus, it is clear that the need to retain information in memory has, in general, a deleterious effect on performance in conceptual tasks. Further, the strategy which minimizes the ordinary mnemonic demands of a problem—focusing— permits much more adequate problem solving, especially when there are extraordinary memory requirements inherent in the task itself.

Availability of Previously Exposed Stimuli

Cahill and Hovland (1960) analyzed the effects of memory factors by comparing the acquisition of concepts under conditions of simultaneous and successive presentation of stimuli. In the simultaneous or "unlimited-memory" condition, all stimuli, once exposed, remained in view for later inspection, whereas in the successive or "limited-memory" condition, each stimulus was removed before the next was presented. The reception paradigm was used, with the subject required to respond to each new stimulus with his best guess of the concept (hypothesis).

Over-all performance was vastly superior in the condition which imposed less severe memory requirements (simultaneous presentation). The data were analyzed to determine the number of (a) perceptual-inference errors (that is, hypotheses which are incompatible with the information in instances which are available for the subject's immediate inspection) and (b) memory errors (that is, hypotheses which are incompatible with previously seen but no longer available instances). Very few errors were attributable to a failure to perceive or to utilize information in perceptually available instances. The greater proportion of errors resulted from a failure to remember earlier instances in a way so as to make the necessary inferences from them. More-over, memory errors occurred with progressively increasing frequency for previously exposed stimuli which were further removed in the series presented. Finally, significant individual differences were observed, with subjects who made more perceptual-inference or memory errors having greater difficulty in acquiring concepts.

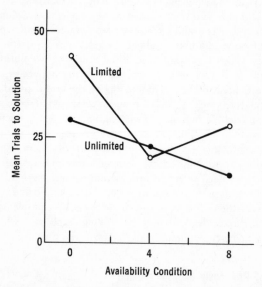

Figure 9. Performance as a function of the number of stimulus patterns available for inspection by subjects working with a limited- (15 seconds) or an unlimited-response time interval. Results are redrawn from Bourne, Goldstein, and Link (1964).

Bourne, Goldstein, and Link (1964) noted that simultaneous and successive presentation methods as used by Cahill and Hovland are the end points of a quantifiable variable called "stimulus availability." Availability may be operationally defined in terms of the number of previously exposed stimuli which a subject may inspect on any trial. In the successive condition *no* previously exposed stimuli are available, while in the simultaneous condition *all* previously exposed stimuli may be inspected. In a series of experiments Bourne *et al.* (1964) varied the number of stimuli, from 0 to 10, which were exposed on any trial. In the first study it was shown that over-all performance generally improves as the number of available stimuli increases from 0 through 5. The facilitative effect was much more significant in problems with a larger number of relevant attributes.

The second experiment encompassed an extended range of availability (up to 10) and showed that performance improves as the number of stimuli increases to 4 but becomes slightly worse with additions beyond this number. The final experiment indicated that the apparent degrading effect of "too much information" was probably a result of a limited-response interval. In the preceding studies subjects were required to respond (formulate a hypothesis) within 15 seconds on each trial. As may be seen in Figure 9, when this limitation was removed performance continued to improve when as many as 8 previously exposed stimuli were available for inspection. Thus, it appears that a certain critical amount of time may be necessary for inspecting and drawing valid conclusions from exposed stimulus instances and that, as the number of available stimuli increases, length of response interval must increase also for maximally efficient utilization of information.

The results of these studies confirm and extend the conclusions of Cahill and Hovland. They show that human memory for previously presented information is not infallible and that the more such information must be retained the poorer is performance. The vast majority of errors are attributable not to inexact inferential processes but to memory failure. The magnitude of memory effects is also a function of task complexity; in simpler tasks, where there is less relevant information to keep track of, memory errors are less frequent and over-all problem solving is more efficient. However, in tasks which are structurally complex, memory demands seriously interfere with the fundamental process of learning or discovering the concept.

Memory Interference from Intervening Stimuli

Cahill and Hovland (1960) showed that incorrect hypotheses stated by a subject were more likely to be incompatible with remote stimuli than with recently presented stimuli. Apparently the information provided by any instance is forgotten in time, an effect which may be attributable to interference caused by subsequently exposed, intervening instances. This outcome, which is predictable from Underwood's analysis (1952) of conceptual problems, has often been demonstrated in other learning tasks. We have noted that such interference processes probably underlie the stimulus sequence effects reported by Kurtz and Hovland (1956).

Hunt (1961) designed several experiments to test directly the interference effect of intervening instances on memory. Subjects were shown a training series of instances sufficient to specify a particular concept. Each instance was indicated by the experimenter to be either positive or negative. After this series, subjects were required to identify as positive or negative each of several unlabeled test instances, using whatever concept they had derived from the training series. The test instances were chosen so that their correct identification depended upon the retention of information provided by a particular "key instance" in the training series. In the first study the key instance was separated from the test series by 1, 3, 5, or 7 intervening instances. In a second study 1, 9, or 17 instances separated the key instance from the test. Finally, in a third experiment, 3 different key instances were positioned in the same training series so that 1, 5, or 9 stimuli separated them from the test series.

The results showed that number of identifications in the test series which are inconsistent with the key instance increases linearly with the number of stimuli intervening between its presentation and the test. Thus, it appears that intervening instances do interfere with the retention of critical information provided by any given stimulus. Presumably a subject attends to and attempts to glean necessary information from each stimulus as it is presented. Concentration on each new stimulus, which is usually different in at least one attribute from others in the series, introduces an element of competition between new and old information. The more such competition the less the chances that old information is retained, resulting in the type of forgetting function observed by Hunt.

Intratrial Forgetting

In Chapter IV, we considered a series of experiments demonstrating the facilitative effect of lengthening postfeedback intervals in a conceptual problem. The results were generally attributable to the opportunity this time provides to assimilate and to make valid inferences from the information given on any trial. With long intervals (20-30 seconds), however, performance suffered. Because neither the stimulus pattern nor its corresponding feedback signal were available for inspection during the postfeedback interval, the possibility arises that the subject forgets increasing amounts of critical information contained in these events as the period is made longer. As a test of this possibility Bourne, Guy, Dodd, and Justesen (1965) compared conditions wherein either the feedback signal, the stimulus pattern, or both were available to the subject throughout a trial with the standard arrangement in which neither is exposed. The conditions yielded roughly equivalent performance levels with short to near optimal interval lengths (1 to 15 seconds). When the interval was increased to 29 seconds, performance got worse for both the standard condition and that wherein only the feedback signal was available. For the two groups which were allowed to inspect the stimulus (that is, stimulus only and stimulus plus feedback signal) throughout each trial, performance was about the same at 15 and 29 seconds of interval length. These results support the hypothesis that long intervals produce intratrial forgetting, especially of information contained in the stimulus. If the necessity to retain the stimulus is eliminated, intratrial learning and therefore over-all performance is benefitted.

MOTIVATION

It is technically difficult to manipulate or to control human motivation. Conditions which arouse and attract human beings are notoriously subject to individual differences and are not well known. Human subjects, moreover, are often not willing or able to submit to the aversive stimulation, for example, electric shock or hunger deprivation, used to study motivational effects in lower animals. Thus, despite the importance of the problem there are very few systematic studies of motivation variables in conceptual behavior.

Anxiety and Generalized Drive States

It is true that anxiety can be aroused by any drive state. Lack of food, water, or social approval may serve to make an organism more or less anxious. Degree of anxiety is in a sense a function of the strength of need or drive for one or more types of incentives. For this reason anxiety is often thought of as a generalized drive or motivational condition; it is not tied to or strictly identified with any single specific need.

Suppose it is true that degree of anxiety tends to be correlated with general level of motivational arousal. Suppose further, as some theorists assert (Spence, 1956), that motivation and learning interact. Motivation potentiates habits or knowledge into action. Then it should be true that anxiety, at least up to a certain level, will facilitate performance in various learning tasks. This argument implies that people who are chronically anxious will perform differently and, up to a point, will perform better than those who are typically more relaxed. This implication has been tested in a number of experiments.

Wesley (1953) compared groups of anxious and normal subjects, selected on the basis of a psychological test (Taylor, 1953), on a series of conceptual problems. The problems required subjects to learn to sort geometric forms on the basis of a single relevant dimension. Anxious subjects showed consistently better performance than nonanxious subjects. They tended to shift solutions from one problem in the series to the next more rapidly and to make fewer perseverative errors, defined as incorrect responses in one problem which would have been correct in the just-preceding problem. Furthermore, the difference between groups increased with each successive problem.

A later study by Romanow (1958) tested a more complicated hypothesis. According to theories which assume an interaction of motivation and learning, an increase in generalized drive or anxiety will enhance the strength of all response tendencies or habits in a subject's repertoire. But response tendencies which are strong to begin with are affected more than weak ones. Consequently, if the correct responses for a conceptual problem are strong, high-drive or highly anxious subjects should perform better than nonanxious subjects. Conversely, if correct response tendencies are weak and interfering responses are strong at the outset, anxious subjects should be inferior on the task to a nonanxious group.

In order to construct conceptual problems with the desired response strength characteristics, Romanow used the procedure and materials devised by Underwood and Richardson (1956a). To solve a problem, the subject had to discover the proper verbal response to be associated with a set of related nouns (the positive instances of a verbal concept). For example, the subject may be required to respond with the adjective "soft" to the nouns "flannel," "kitten," "silk," and "bread." The a priori strength of association—called dominance—between any noun and its descriptive concept may be determined from norms showing the frequency with which each of several adjectives is given as an associate to a particular noun. Strong response tendencies are indexed by high associative frequencies, and conversely, weak tendencies by low frequencies.

In Romanow's experiment high-, intermediate-, and low-anxious groups of subjects learned the proper adjectival responses for six conceptual groupings of four nouns each. Subjects were assigned to groups according to their scores on the Taylor (1953) Anxiety Scale. In any given task all six groupings were of a single degree of dominance—either high, moderate, or low. Nouns were presented serially, using an equivalent of the reception paradigm, and each of the subject's responses was followed by a signal to indicate whether or not it was correct.

The results of this experiment conformed only in part to theoretical expectation. Figure 10 shows that there was little difference among anxiety groups in performance on concept tasks wherein the correct responses were strong at the outset. Theoretically, high-anxious subjects should have been superior. However, the problems used were basically quite simple and were solved in few trials so that a ceiling effect may have masked out group performance differences. On concepts of low dominance, subjects of moderate and low anxiety solved more rapidly and with fewer errors than did high-anxious subjects. Thus, in general, the data may be taken as supporting the

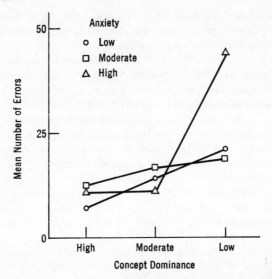

Figure 10. Performance of subjects of high, moderate, and low anxiety on verbal concepts of high, moderate, and low dominance. The major effect of anxiety occurs with low-dominance tasks, whereupon the high-anxiety subjects are significantly inferior to the other two groups. Data from Romanow (1958).

notion that motivational level exerts complex but predictable effects on performance through its interaction with habits or response tendencies.

While it is generally assumed that informative feedback serves primarily to guide a subject toward problem solution, we have noted that some researchers and theorists attribute important reinforcing properties to it as well. Signals which indicate that an incorrect response has been made may be aversive or punishing in some sense, while correct response signals may be seen as positive or rewarding. In most cases it is a matter of judgment (or theoretical commitment) as to whether or not reinforcing effects are carried by the feedback signal.

Wallace (1964) made an attempt to determine the possible reinforcement value of verbal signals, such as "Right" and "Wrong," by comparing performance on concept-learning problems with verbal and nonverbal (in this case a presumably neutral auditory stimulus) feedback. These problems were conducted with the selection paradigm, feedback being provided after each hypothesis about the solution stated by the subject. Each S served under a particular condition determined by combining three levels of feedback intensity (either verbal or nonverbal) with two degrees of problem difficulty. Verbal feedback intensity was manipulated by using statements by the experimenter varying in the degree to which they derogated the subject's performance. For example, the simple statement "Wrong" after a given hypothesis was considered *Mild*, while a remark to the effect, "I don't understand why you can't get the solution" was evaluated as *Strong*. Neutral auditory signals took on three levels of loudness.

Results indicated that any kind of infirming verbal feedback reduced the subject's tendency to offer hypotheses relative to neutral feedback. When "disapproval" emanates from another person rather than some sound-producing apparatus, the subject is more reluctant to guess about the solution. The indication is that negative social feedback can be aversive to a subject. An increase in the intensity of feedback might be expected to produce a corresponding reduction in the number of hypotheses offered by a subject. This result was obtained in the case of nonverbal feedback, but number of hypotheses remained relatively constant over all levels of verbal feedback. Since fewer hypotheses were given in verbal as compared to nonverbal conditions, the failure to observe any trend over intensity levels may simply be due to the necessity to state some minimal number of hypotheses regardless of experimental conditions.

Finally, whereas increasing the intensity of feedback, especially verbal, tended to interfere with performance efficiency in simpler problems, it facilitated performance on complex tasks. If one were to assume that feedback intensity increases the general motivational level of a learner, this result is difficult to rationalize with the aforementioned theories which assume an interactive relationship between habits and drive. Presumably, more difficult tasks are those where correct response tendencies are weak relative to incorrect ones. Thus, increased feedback intensity or increased motivation should have a relatively deleterious effect in these problems. Wallace attributes the observed results to a tendency for highly motivated subjects to shift their responses or response sets more readily. Since difficult problems require such a shift from strong response tendencies to weaker ones, high-intensity feedback facilitates performance in this case. Of course, this explanation was arrived at after the results were obtained and thus is based entirely on post hoc reasoning. Further experimental study will be required before any certain conclusions about the proper explanation will be justified. The important point to be gained for present purposes is that some types of informative feedback may carry more than solution-relevant information to a learner. Verbal feedback, spoken by another person physically present in the same task situation, has effects on performance which differ considerably from those of signals from a neutral source which presumably contain the same fundamental clues to solution. It seems reasonable to assign these added effects to the reinforcing properties of interpersonal communications concerning the adequacy or correctness of the learner's behavior.

Comment

Research on motivational variables in the area of concept learning is obviously in a rather primitive stage. Rigorous studies are few and far between. Several obvious conditions, such as induced motivation, remain to be explored. There are many unanswered questions based on hypotheses arising either from general behavior theories or from experiments in other subareas closely related to conceptual behavior. All of this means that potential relationships between motivation and concept learning should come in for a fair amount of future experimentation.

INTELLIGENCE

It seems only natural that intelligence and the ability to solve conceptual problems should be strongly related. While we usually imply more than an ability to learn and think on a conceptual level when we talk about intelligence, this function is surely an integral part of general intelligence. And, in any plausible definition of intelligence, thinking ability and/or learning ability are invariably mentioned. Standard tests of intellectual functioning, such as the Wechsler Adult Intelligence Scale, include measures of abstraction, such as the adequacy with which a person can pick out the common features of an array of objects and the capacity to deal with both concrete and verbal concepts, almost without exception.

A deeper and more important question than the magnitude of correlation between intelligence and concept learning centers on the underlying processes which contribute to it. Granted that the relationship exists, what are the reasons? Why are people of higher intelligence better at solving conceptual problems? Is there something basically different about the way in which people of high and low intelligence learn or solve problems? These are among the questions studied in a series of recent experiments reported by Osler and others (for example, Osler and Fivel, 1961). The results provide some interesting answers but also contain important theoretical implications and suggestions for further research.

Intelligence and Rate of Learning Concepts

As a first step in their study Osler and Fivel administered the Wechsler Intelligence Scale for Children to a large number of subjects. On the basis of these test scores two groups of children, one with IQ's between 90 and 109 and another with IQ's above 110, were selected at each of three ages; namely, six, ten, and fourteen years. A variation of the reception paradigm was used in the conceptual task, and the subject was given a marble (reinforcer) for each correct response. The stimulus patterns presented to subjects were portrayals of naturalistic objects, such as a flower or a basket, on the assumption that such stimuli are more familiar and discriminable for children than geometric designs or other formal stimuli.

Both age and intelligence were associated with more rapid concept learning. To explore more deeply the behavioral mechanisms which underly these findings, the performance of individual subjects was examined. Some subjects seemed to learn or improve gradually over a series of trials while others showed a sudden, almost insightful, solution. This was taken as an indication that some subjects mastered the task through the acquisition of S-R associations while others attained solution by testing discrete hypotheses. The relative frequency of gradual and sudden learners was a direct function of intelligence. At all ages the frequency of sudden learners was much higher among the high-IQ subjects. According to the authors this finding may mean that brighter subjects are relatively better able to use symbolic or mediational processes in their efforts to solve a problem. Whereas normal subjects at these ages may learn according to a gradual acquisition of S-R associations, more intelligent subjects presumably use the higher-level approach of actively formulating and testing hypotheses until the solution is discovered.

The results of this experiment and the interpretation given to them are reminiscent of some earlier work by Kendler and Kendler (1959). These experimenters compared the performance of young children on reversal and nonreversal shifts and found that fast learners, that is, those who made fewer than the average number of errors on an initial problem, solved the reversal more rapidly than the nonreversal shift. Just the opposite result obtained with slow learners. Kendler and Kendler pointed out that a theory which assumes the gradual formation of direct associations between physical stimuli and overt responses predicts better performance on nonreversal as opposed to reversal shifts and therefore accounts reasonably well for the behavior of slower learners. On the other hand, a mediated S-R theory—which assumes the formation and utilization of internal symbolic representations of previously learned habits—predicts better performance on reversal problems and provides a more adequate interpretation of the behavior of faster learners. The faster learners, according to Kendler and Kendler, were acting on the basis of internal, mediational processes (hypotheses?) during the shift problem. They reasoned that all normal human beings eventually develop the capacity for this level of functioning, since a parallel study (Kendler and D'Amato, 1955) had shown that for adult subjects the reversal shift is almost invariably easier than the nonreversal. The children in this experiment may have been of an age at which the mediational activities appropriate to the task were just beginning to take shape. Some subjects, that is, the faster learners, were further along in this development than others. In any case, if the faster learners were in fact more intelligent on the average than the slower learners, the results are quite consistent with those of Osler and Fivel. In both cases the utilization of mediational activity during concept learning, which results in notable differences in overt behavior and in the way the problem is solved, is more characteristic of brighter, more intelligent individuals.

Intelligence and the Complexity of Stimuli

Suppose it is true that children of high and low intelligence go about solving conceptual problems in characteristically different ways. Then there are certain variables which should affect the performance of these subjects differently. Experiments designed to explore the interaction of these variables with intelligence could serve to supply corroborative evidence on the validity of an interpretation which attributes different mechanisms of conceptual functioning to different subjects, and to clarify the actual role that intelligence plays in problem solving.

One variable which may affect the performance of gradual and sudden learners differently is stimulus complexity. For those children who approach a concept problem by testing hypotheses, speed of solving should be reduced by increasing the number of irrelevant dimensions of the stimuli because each dimension adds a certain number of hypotheses that may be tested. Those children who solve by gradually acquiring S-R associations may show no such effect because the number of associations between levels on the relevant dimension and response categories is unaffected by the number of irrelevant dimensions. Osler and Trautman (1961) tested this prediction. Stimulus materials of two complexity levels were used. The less complex set consisted of black circles in varying number on a white background; the more complex stimuli were multicolored naturalistic objects in varying number, which clearly involved many more dimensions than did the circles. In both sets subjects of two intelligence levels (namely, IQ between 90 and 109 and IQ above 110) at each of three age levels (namely, six, ten, and fourteen years) were required to identify the concept "twoness"—all stimuli containing two objects were positive instances.

Within each age level the results show a reliable difference between more and less complex stimuli for subjects of higher intelligence but no difference for the normal group. The findings are then consistent with the interpretation that high intelligence in children is associated with mediational symbolic activity which presumably takes the form of hypothesis testing, while children of normal intelligence learn by gradual association. It may be, as Kendler and Kendler have argued, that children within the age range studied here are in a transitional stage from a direct S-R associational capability to a more complex capability involving internalized, symbolic functioning. The more intelligent subjects are simply more advanced in this development, and thus some or all of them perform in a mediational fashion. If so, we should expect to observe more of a difference between stimulus complexity conditions for normal subjects as age increases. Or, to put it differently, except perhaps for an over-all difference in rate of learning, the normal and high intelligence groups should come more to resemble each other in their relative levels of performance in the two complexity conditions with increasing age. In fact, this is what the data of Osler and Trautman show.

Intelligence and the Specificity of Task-Related Instructions

Osler and her collaborators gave very general instructions to subjects about the task. The fact that superior subjects acted like hypothesis testers while average subjects did not may have been the result of certain self-instructional activities. The brighter subjects may have supplemented the experimenter's instructions by directing themselves to seek for consistencies between feedback and dimensional properties of the stimuli while the average subjects worked without self-instructions until reinforcement strengthened differential response tendencies to exemplars and nonexemplars of the concept. In an effort to study this possibility Osler and Weiss (1962) designed two experiments. The first was a direct replication of Osler and Fivel (1961), using very general instructions to subjects. The second was essentially the same except that instructions specifically directed subjects to search for and test hypotheses. As before, six groups of subjects were used in each experiment, two (high and average intelligence) at each of three ages (six, ten, and fourteen years).

Instructions to test hypotheses reduced the difference in performance due to intelligence to a negligible amount. Thus, it seems possible to manipulate the strategy or problem solving mechanism through preliminary guidance. The result also points to the fact that more intelligent subjects are probably equipped with a greater capacity to guide their own problem solving efforts.

Comment

Much remains to be learned about the relationship between intelligence and conceptual behavior. For example, it is commonly accepted that intelligence is a composite of several, perhaps many, specific abilities, such as numerical ability, verbal ability, and the like. Do these various abilities all relate to conceptual behavior? What are their specific roles in the process? Further, most of the studies reported here deal exclusively with young children. What about adult intelligence? Do the same findings hold with children and adults? The interpretations of Osler and Kendler, which point to the important growth of mediational abilities with age, would suggest that they do not.

PERCEPTUAL PROCESSES

A subject must perceive correctly the information available in a stimulus or a feedback signal before he can learn or make valid inferences from it. In a sense, perception of stimulation initiates the chain of events leading to a conceptual response and eventually to problem solution. Knowledge of the perceptual activity required by and involved in a problem, then, is vital to a complete understanding of conceptual behavior.

Perception and an S-R Analysis of Concept Learning

A major factor controlling the perceptual activities of an organism is his attention or orientation to the stimulus field. Kendler, Glucksberg, and Keston (1961) described the behavioral events on any trial of a conceptual problem as a chain which begins with an orienting response (triggered by some "ready" signal). The stimulus, as perceived, then elicits a mediational or symbolic response which serves as a cue to the overt act of categorizing. The mediational response, as we have noted earlier, is essentially an abstraction of certain stimulus attributes. Eventually, when the relevant attributes have been abstracted, mediational activities provide the internal stimulation to which correct category responses are associated.

Kendler *et al.* developed an experimental procedure permitting independent control over the orienting and mediating responses within the behavioral chain. The subjects (college students) were required to solve two successive concept problems. Problem 2 was a reversal shift for half the subjects and a nonreversal shift for the others. Recall that reversals are easier than nonreversals for adult subjects and that the S-R explanation is based on the assertion that a nonreversal shift requires the formation of a new mediational link while a reversal does not. For half the subjects within the two shift conditions, the required perceptual-orienting response in Problem 1 was also appropriate in Problem 2. For the remaining subjects a different orienting response was involved in Problem 2. This was accomplished by flashing two geometrical designs on the viewing screen simultaneously and far enough apart so that the subject could not see both at once. The task was to learn how to categorize patterns presented on either the right or the left side of the screen. Thus the subject had to discover first which patterns to attend to and then the correct scheme for classifying them. For those subjects allowed to use the same perceptual response, patterns on the same side of the screen carried the relevant information in both problems. The side was changed for the other subjects. As is typical in solution-shift experiments, Problem 2 began without interruption after the subject reached a high performance criterion on Problem 1.

A marked difference in shift performance in the four conditions was observed. Scores on the reversal problem for subjects using the same (Problem 1) perceptual response were significantly better than those in any other condition. There were no differences among the remaining groups. This result is consistent with a mediated S-R analysis. Superior performance was associated with that condition wherein the appropriate perceptual and mediational responses for Problem 2 had been preestablished and were available at the time of the shift. Subjects in the other groups had to learn either new perceptual or mediational responses or both. The fact that performance was about the same in these groups indicates that the existence of one appropriate link in the behavioral chain without the other is of little advantage. This finding may mean either that new perceptual and mediational responses can be learned concurrently (or nearly so) or that appropriate responses in the chain may extinguish for lack of consistent reinforcement during the period in which a replacement is being learned for the inappropriate link.

The Correctness of Perceptual Responses

A study by Cahill and Hovland (1960) supplied some informative data on the accuracy of perceptual responses in a concept-learning problem. In the analysis of data two types of erroneous responses (verbalized hypotheses in this case) were identified: those resulting from a failure to retain information available in previously seen stimulus patterns (memory errors) and those attributable to a failure to make proper use of information available in exposed stimulus patterns. The latter were labeled perceptual-inference errors to indicate either a faulty perception of the stimulus or the drawing of some invalid inference from it. It was noted earlier that perceptual-inference errors were rare, with subjects making an average of slightly more than one in approximately 20 trials. However, there were large individual differences, and not unexpectedly, those subjects who were prone to this type of error had greater difficulty in solving the conceptual problem. Subjects who made no perceptual errors attained solutions significantly more rapidly than those who made one or more.

Ordered Versus Random Stimulus Arrays

In the last two sections we considered studies which show how perception affects the correctness of the subject's overt category responses or hypotheses and determines his success in solving problems. In this and the next section we shall review some experiments wherein variables which affect the ease of making correct perceptual responses are manipulated. The results will demonstrate that such manipulations have very definite effects not only on the over-all efficiency of conceptual behavior but also on the plans or strategies adopted in an effort to arrive at problem solution.

The first investigation, reported by Bruner et al. (1956), used the selection paradigm and dealt with the orderliness of the array of stimuli presented to the subject. Each subject solved a series of four conjunctive problems. For half the subjects, the population of stimulus patterns was laid out randomly, while for the other subjects the arrangement of cards was quite systematic. In the systematic layout all cards with small figures appeared on one side while those with large figures appeared on the other side; black figures were presented in the upper half of the array and yellow ones in the bottom half. Divisions on the remaining four dimensions were similarly made with the general result that any two neighboring cards differed in one and only one attribute. Perceptually, the two arrays were quite different, the orderly layout appearing to be highly patterned and the random arrangement looking like a patchwork quilt. One might expect that subjects who worked with the random array would be more likely to adopt a conservative focusing strategy in an effort to overcome the difficulties the array created for keeping track of positive and negative instances and of the potentially relevant attributes. However, several factors militate against focusing under this condition. First, the random array makes it hard to locate stimuli needed for testing; that is, stimuli which differ from the initial card only on certain attributes. Second, the random array introduces more opportunity for forgetting what has been learned on earlier trials because of the interference that arises during the process of scanning for particular stimuli. Finally, the structure of the random array simply does not induce the systematic testing of attributes required of conservative focusers. Rather, the layout is such as to suggest a haphazard approach to problem solving. Keeping track of particular instances and of potentially relevant attributes is, by the nature of things, easier with the orderly array.

Subjects working with the orderly layout took significantly fewer trials to learn (about 40% less than in the random condition). The orderly group solved the problem in nearly the minimum possible number of trials. Their card selections suggested strongly the use of conservative focusing. Members of the random group showed more of a tendency to test independent hypotheses about solution by a successive scanning technique. Further, they chose a larger number of redundant stimuli, as is characteristic of the scanning strategy. The data clearly show that a perceptual variable, that is, orderliness of the stimulus population, has both quantitative and qualitative effects on performance. It determines not only over-all efficiency of problem solving but also the strategy adopted in an attempt to bring about solution.

Compact Versus Distributed Stimulus Displays

The geometric designs, commonly used as stimulus materials in concept-learning experiments, are compact in the sense that all (or most) stimulus attributes are embodied in a single figure. The subject may perceive the various attributes, each arising from a different dimension, in a single glance. It is possible, however, to distribute or spread the attributes of a stimulus pattern over several spatially separate figures or objects. For example, Neisser and Weene (1962) used consonant clusters as stimuli and required the identification of concepts based on the presence or absence of one or two letters in each cluster. It is difficult to know which type of stimulus arrangement is easier to work with. On the one hand, distributed stimuli may facilitate problem solving by calling the subject's attention more forcefully to the various independent stimulus attributes. Certainly it is not easy to overlook any attribute in a distributed display. Yet, there may be an advantage to compact stimuli in the sense that the subject can perceive its various attributes without the necessity of scanning a series of figures.

The question was explored in a study by Shepard, Hovland, and Jenkins (1961). They constructed conceptual problems with formally identical solutions using three types of stimulus displays. The patterns used are illustrated in Figure 11 and may be labeled compact, distributed-different dimensions,

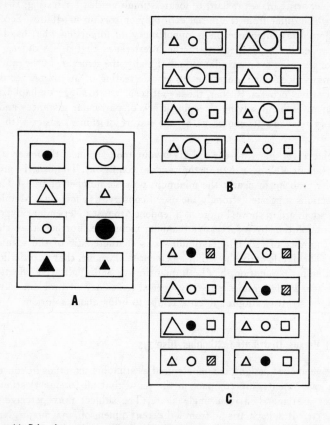

Figure 11. Stimulus patterns illustrating three different types of perceptual representations. All three types are based on three dimensions, each with two values. Type A is compact; the three dimensions are Color (black-white), Size (large-small), and Shape (circle-triangle). Type B is distributed-same dimension; all three elements of each pattern (triangle, circle, and square) vary in the same dimension—Size. Type C is distributed-different dimensions; each pattern element varies in a unique way—Size, Color, and Cross-hatching (present-absent). Redrawn from Shepard, Hovland, and Jenkins (1961).

and distributed-same dimension. The task required subjects both to learn how to sort patterns correctly and to formulate a verbal description of the solution. Subjects performed better almost invariably with compact than with either type of distributed display. The performance difference between the two distributed types was small and unreliable but tended to favor patterns in which different dimensions characterized each figure.

Shepard *et al.* indicated that at least two factors determined the result. One is the relative difficulty subjects have in translating distributed stimuli into words. Whereas a compact stimulus may be verbalized as "a large black triangle," the corresponding description of a distributed stimulus might be "figure one-large, figure two-black, figure three-triangle." This in turn makes for longer, more complicated statements of any concept which is composed of two or more relevant attributes. Thus, sheer length of verbal description may account in part for the greater difficulty of learning concepts with distributed stimulus displays. Another possibility is based more directly on the perceptual characteristics of these displays. We have noted that distributed stimuli tend to force subjects to deal with the attributes individually, while combinations of attributes are more obvious in compact stimuli. The solution to problems which require a conjunction of attributes (for example, black triangle), such as those used in this experiment, may be more easily perceived in compact as opposed to distributed displays.

Changing the perceptual characteristics of a stimulus display affects the efficiency of information utilization in conceptual problems. Whether the outcome is the direct result of perceptual factors, such as the ease or difficulty of "seeing" the relevant attributes, or is a consequence of some indirect action of perceptual characteristics on verbalizing and/or remembering, is difficult to determine. This remains a significant question for future research.

TRANSFER OF TRAINING

Transfer of training may be described as the influence of prior learning or experience in one task on performance in another. It refers to the utilization of habits, associations, or knowledge acquired under one set of circumstances in a new, later situation. Depending on the characteristics of the original learning and transfer tasks, the effects that carry-over may be positive (facilitory), negative (inhibitory), or negligible. Performance on the second task may be better than, worse than, or no different from what it would have been without practice on the first. Transfer has been of considerable interest to psychologists for a variety of reasons. If any example is needed one may point to the fundamental place of transfer effects in education. Instruction and practice with the variety of problems encountered "on the job" can hardly be provided during formal training. One way to evaluate the effectiveness of an educational experience is to determine the extent to which it transfers positively to other situations.

While the extensive results of experiments on transfer are not easy to summarize, it is probably correct to say that two broad classes of conditions are involved. On the one hand are the relationships that hold between the specific stimulus, response, and associational features of two tasks. The similarity of response components, for example, has a reliable and well-known influence on both direction and amount of transfer. In addition, there appears to be a second, more general, basis for transfer in the rules or principles which are common to a class of problems. We have seen how performance improves dramatically over a series of tasks structured around the same rule (Harlow, 1959; Freibergs and Tulving, 1961). The learning and transfer that take place transcend effects attributable to specific stimulus and response features of any two tasks in the series. The important element is the rule and the response sequences or strategies which the subject acquires for implementing the rule. Both factors may be seen to operate in the experiments which are summarized in this section.

Degree of Original Learning

In conceptual problems information feedback to the subject serves the function of confirming or infirming his current mode of responding. A "correct-response" signal from the experimenter presumably either increases the subject's tendency to make the same category response to the same stimulus pattern on some later trial or supports whatever hypothesis he presently entertains about solution. An "error" conversely weakens response tendencies. It is reasonable to suppose that the more confirmation a subject receives for a given way of responding the more certain he becomes of the solution. An interesting question then arises about the subject's readiness or ability to shift his mode of response as is required in a second, transfer problem. How is the ease of a shift from one solution to a second affected by degree of confirmation or degree of learning on the first? If one were to generalize from experiments performed in simpler learning situations, such as conditioning, he would probably expect the shift to be more difficult as degree of original learning increases. It is common to find that a larger number of reinforcements (confirmations of a given response) leads to a greater persistence of that response when reinforcement is withdrawn or changed. But such studies are not entirely analogous to the circumstances that obtain in a conceptual problem, and a direct experimental approach to the problem is necessary to answer the question.

Two apposite investigations were reported by Grant and co-workers (Grant and Berg, 1948; Grant and Cost, 1954). Both were based on the Wisconsin Card Sorting Test (WCST), which requires the subject to discover

the one dimension from a total of three—color, form, and number of figures—
that is relevant to sorting stimulus cards into four categories. The subject is
required to make a certain number of correct responses in a row to indicate
his knowledge of the relevant dimension. After this criterion is attained the
basis of sorting cards is changed without any interruption or warning, and
the subject is required to solve a new problem or to identify a new relevant
dimension. Similar shifts in solution may be introduced repeatedly, and in
these experiments, the subject was required to change his basis of sorting
the cards five times. The main variable in the experiments was the number
of confirmations given for one solution before the shift to a new one was put
into effect. In the first study (Grant and Berg, 1948) seven different groups
of subjects were required to make 3, 4, 5, 6, 7, 8, or 10 correct responses in
a row prior to each shift. In the second study (Grant and Cost, 1954) groups
made 5, 10, 20, or 40 correct responses prior to each shift. The greater the
number of consecutive confirmations of a given problem solution (3 through
40 trials), the better the subject's over-all performance and the more rapid
his shift to a new solution when required. Moreover, numbers of perseverative
errors, that is, incorrect responses on any problem which would have been
correct in the preceding problem, also decreased with number of preshift
confirmations. As such the data appear to be contrary to the principle
that response persistence increases with number of reinforcements (or confirming feedback signals). The authors, however, attributed this inconsistency
to the complexity of conceptual behavior relative to the conditioning situations in which the reinforcement principle has gained its foremost support.
Grant argued that the clarity of a solution increases with degree of learning.
The subject's readiness to change his mode of responding depends on his
ability to discriminate the shift in feedback from one dimension to another.
The ease of this discrimination is a function of how much confirmation has
been supplied for the preshift solution.

Multiple- and Single-Problem Training

We have seen several examples of strong positive transfer when subjects
practice and solve a series of problems each based on the same fundamental
principle or rule. Typically, in these experiments, the stimulus aspects change
from problem to problem, although the rule is consistent. Adams (1954) noted
that the multiple-problem method used in this research is only one of several
possible training techniques. He proceeded to design an experiment to determine the relative effectiveness of a multiple-problem routine as contrasted
with training which involved repeated presentation of the same problem;
that is, training wherein the rule and the relevant stimulus features remained
constant throughout.

Adams prepared a set of four-category problems in which the solution
depended upon the relative location in a stimulus display of two different

forms; for example, squares and circles. The same rule held for all problems, although the forms themselves varied from problem to problem. One group of subjects was trained on 24 distinct problems (forms changing), being given only 8 trials on each. A second group was trained for the same total number of trials (192) on the stimuli of a single problem (forms constant). After training, both groups were transferred to a new problem (new forms, same solution rule) and were given 24 trials in which to solve. Performance during training trials, as measured by percentage of correct responses, was better in the single-problem condition. Such a result is not unexpected in view of the fact that subjects had ample opportunity to memorize the necessary stimuli-response associations. The critical test was provided by the transfer problem. Here it was observed that over-all performance was again better after single-problem training, although a larger percentage of correct responses on the first few transfer trials was shown by the multiple-problem group. Thus, while multiple-problem training does produce considerable facility in solving problems of a given type and also has the advantage of effecting a smoother transition from one problem to another (as shown by performance on the early trials of the transfer test), Adams concluded that single-problem training is in general superior in the development of proficiency in problem solving.

Noting the apparent discrepancy between these findings and the conclusions typically drawn from learning set experiments, Callantine and Warren (1955) pointed out the strong possibility that 8 trials may not have been sufficient for learning in the problems used by Adams, which surely would inhibit performance in his multiple-problem group. If this were the case, it could account for the inferiority of this training condition relative to the single-problem condition. To explore this possibility, Callantine and Warren conducted a follow-up experiment. Subjects were trained for 80 trials on a four-category conceptual problem in which the relevant dimensions were color and form of geometric designs. For some subjects a different stimulus pattern (20 belonging to each of the four categories) was presented on each trial. For another group each of 40 patterns (10 per category) was repeated twice during training. In still other conditions, 16 (4 per category), 8 (2 per category), and 4 (1 per category) patterns repeated 5, 10, and 20 times, respectively, made up the stimuli during the 80 training trials. On these trials the subject was required to guess until he named the correct category for each pattern. After training, all subjects were presented with a transfer problem consisting of 80 new stimulus patterns which were to be categorized on the basis of the principle learned during training.

While performance during training was retarded by increasing the number of different stimulus patterns, just the opposite trend was observed in the transfer problem. The larger the number of training stimuli presented, the greater the amount of positive transfer. Thus, the results provide an example, contrary to Adams, of facilitated transfer by training on multiple problems (multiple stimulus examples of the conceptual rule). Callantine and

Warren attribute the difference between their results and Adams' to procedural variables and to the fact that solution to the training problem was attained by all subjects in their study but not in Adams'. They further assert that bases of better transfer from multiple-problem (stimuli) training derives from the acquisition of a more general or generalizable solution. The greater the breadth of experience during training, the better equipped the learner is to handle new problems and new stimulus materials. Thus, the data suggest that two factors enter into determining the degree of positive transfer: (a) a high degree of learning on the individual problems and (b) the presentation of a sufficient number of problems to insure a general solution (that is, rule learning).

Morrisett and Hovland (1959) performed an experiment which gives further support to the foregoing conclusion. They hypothesized that a training condition intermediate between Adams' multiple-problem and single-problem procedures would do best of all, for subjects would be exposed to a variety of stimuli and yet would be given sufficient practice with each to achieve a moderate to high degree of learning. All subjects were given 192 training trials. Group I worked throughout on a single problem consisting of the repeated (48 times) presentation of four different stimulus patterns (geometric designs) each belonging to one of four response categories. Group II was trained on 24 different problems (different sets of four patterns) and was given 8 trials on each. Group III was trained for 64 trials on each of 3 problems. The rule for responding was the same in all problems, being based on four possible positional arrangements of two different forms. Following training, all subjects were given 24 trials on the same test problem.

The data shown in Figure 12 revealed an improvement in performance for all subjects over the training period with Groups I and III both showing more rapid learning than Group II. In accord with expectations Group III, whose training provided both a high degree of learning within a problem and generalized experience with several problems, made fewest errors during transfer. However, consistent with Adams' results, better transfer was observed from single-problem (Group I) than from multiple-problem (Group II) training, which indicates that a high degree of learning even within one problem is a more important determiner of transfer than breadth of experience with different examples of the concepts. It should be noted that the superiority of Group III over Group I in transfer is entirely limited to the first few trials. Group I performance on the transfer problem improved rapidly and was the equivalent of that in Group III after about 8 trials. The evidence provided by Morrisett and Hovland reconciles the apparent discrepancy in earlier experiments. When, as in the Callantine and Warren study, a high degree of learning on each problem (or concept example) is insured, transfer improves with the number of problems. If, however, the presentation of many problems reduces concomitantly the amount of practice on each, transfer may suffer. Morrisett and Hovland explain the importance of both intraproblem learning

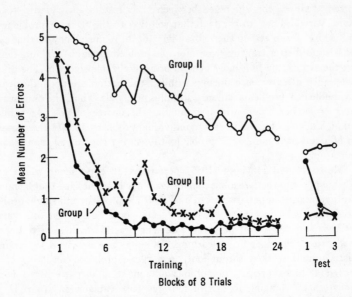

Figure 12. Mean errors per block of 8 trials made during training and transfer problems by subjects in the Morrisett and Hovland (1959) experiment. The superiority of Group III with respect to Group II during transfer is largely limited to the first few trials.

and breadth of problem experience in terms of their contributions to (*a*) strength of relevant stimulus-response associations and (*b*) the development of a rule for responding which is indifferent to the particular stimulus forms used in any single problem.

Transfer of Part Solutions to Compound Concepts

Theoretically any number of stimulus attributes may be relevant to a given concept. One may think of each attribute as a simple concept in itself as well as a part of a more complex, compound principle. Kendler and Vineberg (1954) explored the extent of transfer from learning the subparts of a compound concept to performance on the compound itself. The experiment involved three groups of subjects each of which learned successively two simple (unidimensional) concepts and a compound test concept. Group II learned both simple concepts from which the test problem was constructed; Group I learned only one part of the compound during training (the second training problem was irrelevant to the transfer task); and Group O learned neither concept involved in the transfer problem. Because performance on the compound depended on two specific response tendencies (one for each relevant attribute) it would be expected on the basis of S-R theory that previous training with these tendencies would facilitate later performance. Therefore, learning on the transfer problem should be directly related to number of relevant simple concepts learned during training.

During the two training problems subjects were required to sort a deck of cards, displaying geometric designs, into two categories according to a single dimension of the designs. For example, the solution may be to place large figures in one category and small ones in the other. On the compound problem the subject sorted the same cards into four categories now on the basis of the four conjunctive combinations of two relevant dimensions; for example, (1) small-rectilinear, (2) large-rectilinear, (3) small-curved, and (4) large-curved figures. Consistent with predictions, transfer was directly related to the number of relevant concepts learned during training. Kendler and Vineberg interpreted these results to mean that the essential learning which is basic to performance in these tasks entails a complex association between external stimuli and overt category responses mediated by internal (and probably) verbal activity. That is, physical stimuli elicit within the subject a verbal (descriptive?) response. This activity in turn serves as a cue for the sorting response made to the stimulus. The advantage in transfer derived from the acquisition of appropriate simple concepts does not stem, then, from mere repetition of correct sorting responses but, rather, from the opportunity provided by initial training for the necessary verbal responses to become dominant. Unlike simple conditioning, in which practice trials presumably increase the strength of S-R connections, training in concept problems determines which verbal cues are dominant. If the appropriate cues are strengthened during training, transfer will be facilitated. We have seen a similar argument used by Kendler (see Chapter III) in his interpretation of other transfer situations particularly those involving reversal and non-reversal shifts. This problem is considered once again in the next section.

Types of Problem Shifts

A nonreversal shift in problem solution requires the subject to change his basis for categorizing stimulus patterns from one dimension to another. A reversal shift changes the pattern-category assignments while maintaining the same relevant dimension. Research has provided a reasonably clear picture of the effects of these shift types on performance. With nonverbal organisms, such as rats and preverbal children, the nonreversal is an easier shift than the reversal. However, just the opposite result obtains with verbal children and adults (Kendler and Kendler, 1962). These findings, as we have seen, have important theoretical implications. A nonmediated theory, assuming the formation of direct associations between physical stimuli and overt responses (Spence, 1936), predicts the effects observed with lower organisms. However, some sort of mediational elaboration of S-R theory, which admits to the operation of internal, symbolic activities, is often proposed as an account of the findings with articulate organisms. Kendler and Kendler (1959) have studied the performance of children in the transitional stage of mediational (verbal) development and have shown that those who are further along in the process (that is, brighter or more mature) are more likely to find the reversal problem easier.

There is another plausible explanation for better performance in a reversal problem (Buss, 1953) based on knowledge of partial reinforcement effects. Suppose in Problem 1 the subject learns to sort red patterns into Category 1 and blue ones into Category 2. A nonreversal shift to form as a relevant dimension might require the placement of squares in Category 1 and triangles in Category 2. But half the squares are red and half the triangles are blue. Therefore, 50% of the time during shift trials, the first solution will be confirmed or reinforced. This is obviously not true for the reversal shift. Continued (partial) reinforcement or confirmation of the first solution may interfere with discovery of the new solution in a nonreversal relative to a reversal shift.

One way to determine the importance of partial reinforcement in shift performance is to devise an experimental technique to eliminate it in a nonreversal shift. If, under such conditions, the reversal-nonreversal difference vanishes one would conclude that partial reinforcement provides an adequate explanation for the typical results. If the difference remains then presumably the mediational hypothesis would gain support.

Although several have been tried, the most adequate technique for eliminating partial reinforcement was devised by Harrow and Friedman (1958). In a conventional card-sorting task, subjects were assigned to the usual reversal and nonreversal conditions. Partial reinforcement of the first concept after a nonreversal shift was eliminated by using different sets of stimulus cards in the two problems. This results in a situation in which subjects are never reinforced during Problem 2 for a specific stimulus-response association acquired during Problem 1. For example, suppose the subject learned to sort stimuli on the basis of the number dimension during Problem 1, the patterns containing *one* or *two* figures which are either *red* or *green* in color. In a nonreversal shift to color, the cards are changed so that the number of figures appearing on each is either *three* or *four*. Thus in Problem 2 the subject no longer has an opportunity to respond to single-figure or double-figure stimulus patterns, thereby precluding the partial reinforcement of Problem 1 associations. A similar arrangement can be effected if the subject learns color first and shifts to number relevant. Experimental results based on this technique were clear and definitive. Reversal shifts were significantly easier than nonreversals, even with partial reinforcement eliminated. While the data are hardly sufficient to prove the validity of any single theoretical position, they do cast doubt on the partial reinforcement argument presented by Buss.

Although the data from the foregoing studies of solution shifts seem clear cut and readily interpretable, they by no means represent the full range of complexity of this issue. Other recent experiments, contrary to S-R theory, indicate that (a) number of response categories affects the relative difficulty of reversal and nonreversal shifts (Ludvigson and Caul, 1964) and (b) transfer, even for a reversal, may be negative (Isaacs and Duncan, 1962). Results like these point up some of the important problems of transfer which are yet to be solved.

Preestablished Sets

Human subjects often enter a laboratory task with preestablished response tendencies, expectations, or sets. These sets are based on past experiences in similar or related situations. Because experiences differ among individuals, so do their sets. Sometimes a set is appropriate to the task, and sometimes it is inappropriate. Performance in the laboratory may be facilitated or inhibited accordingly. To study the problem carefully, we would want to devise and use a laboratory-controlled method of producing sets rather than to rely on presumptions about a subject's extralaboratory experience. All studies we have discussed in this section are, in the broadest sense, studies of laboratory-controlled set. The subject first learns one way of responding to a population of stimuli—establishing the set; then the influence of this learning on subsequent performance is observed. There is another type of experimental paradigm for the study of set which has seen some use in problem solving research. In it the subject is given preliminary experience in one context which may bear little or no obvious relationship to the problem he will subsequently be asked to solve. However, embedded within this preliminary experience are certain clues or hints which may be useful in the later problem. The question then arises as to whether or not the preliminary experience is sufficient to activate response tendencies which guide subsequent attempts at problem solving.

This procedure was employed by Gelfand (1958). His subjects served in two ostensibly independent work sessions. In the first they memorized a serial list of "set-inducing" words, while in the second (conducted several hours later) they were required to solve a four-category conceptual problem. During Session 1 independent groups of subjects learned a list comprised of words which were associated with (R) the relevant attributes, (I) the irrelevant attributes of the concept problem, or (N) neither. The words of conditions R and I, while related, did not include the actual common names of any attributes used in later problems. In Session 2 these groups were further subdivided such that an equal number of subjects from each solved a problem with 2 relevant and either 0, 2, or 4 irrelevant dimensions, thus providing three points on the continuum of problem complexity. In accord with expectations those subjects who learned a list of words denoting the relevant dimensions performed best in the later conceptual task. Moreover, the degree of facilitation increased with problem complexity. However, learning a list of words descriptive of irrelevant dimensions did not interfere, since performance in conditions I and N did not differ. Three results are summarized in Figure 13. The author further reports that no subject detected

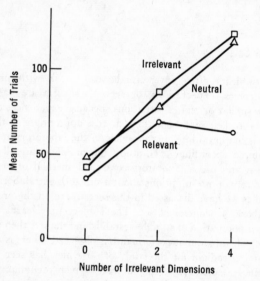

Figure 13. Performance on conceptual tasks of three degrees of complexity as a function of type of set-inducing pretraining. Preliminary experience with words associated with relevant stimulus attributes facilitates performance relative to neutral or irrelevant pretraining. Data from Gelfand (1958).

any connection between the two experimental sessions. Thus it does appear possible under some circumstances to induce in subjects a mild set to respond to certain features of a stimulus complex through prior training in a seemingly unrelated context.

VERBAL CONCEPTS

The interplay of language and human conceptual behavior, though exceedingly complex, is a fundamental issue—it pervades most, if not all, of the theory and research with which this book is concerned. That verbal processes enter into the chain of behaviors appropriate in almost any conceptual problem is an indisputable fact. We use words as overt signs or labels (a code) for physical entities or events; words serve as symbols on a covert or implicit level; they supply (as mediators) self-generated stimulation or cues to overt responses; singly or in sequential combination they provide a frame for retaining and communicating information. Language assists in our efforts to deal and contend with a potentially overpowering real world of varying and unique objects. Among other important functions it constitutes the essential system and the tools of human conceptual activity. While it is possible to argue for the evolution of a linguistic system on this utilitarian basis, some have gone still further to a position which claims that language determines completely the *whats* and *hows* of all mature human behavior, including thinking and the conceptual processes.

The study of verbal learning and verbal behavior is an expansive enterprise which has occupied psychologists for many years. In simple terms it concerns the way in which human beings learn to produce linguistic responses, to associate them with environmental events, and to integrate them sequentially so as to express coherent and meaningful messages. Inevitably, this work has converged on and frequently overlapped research on human conceptual activities. Consider the definitions given in Chapter II. There we showed that it is possible to analyze any specific concept into its component rule(s) and relevant attribute(s). There is a tempting analogy here to the structure of a language. Is it not reasonable to liken words (the lexicon) to the attributes of concepts? A word indeed represents one behavioral (functional) response to a discriminable feature of the environment. A word is a coded reaction to stimulation. The color red and the word "red" have an obvious relationship which may make the analogy useful. One may even go further to contend that the lexicon of names is merely a consensually valid mapping or translation of the world of nonverbal stimulation into words. But the language, of course, is more than mere names. There are certain principles, a grammar or syntax, which govern the way in which descriptive sounds are ordered or arranged for purposes of expressing actions, functions, relations, and the like. And indeed there are words—prepositions, conjunctions —devoid of naming properties, which serve to implement these principles. It makes a certain amount of sense to think of these principles as counterparts of conceptual rules. A rule combines given attributes in some way so as to prescribe a meaningful specific grouping of objects. A grammatical principle generates an ordering of given words (names, descriptors) so as to prescribe some understandable specific message concerning the referents. Attributes are the particular, usually point-at-able, qualities of things; words are their signs or labels. A conceptual rule is a vehicle for generating sensible stimulus groupings, given a set of attributes; likewise grammatical rules generate a meaningful ordering of words.

Like all analogies this one readily admits to overextention. There is no implication here of an identity of linguistic and conceptual systems. While the existence of common or at least parallel features may be granted, we should also recognize the essential independence of these processes. We should not deny, without considerable evidence, for example, the inarticulate organism's ability to learn and respond to stimulus groupings. Our main aim here is to point up (*a*) the similarity of behavioral components of verbal and conceptual learning, and (*b*) the symbolic and response systems provided by language and within which conceptual behavior may manifest itself. Even those conceptual problems for which the stimulus (for example, geometric designs) and response (for example, button presses) are devoid of verbal content are likely to be translated by the adult human organism into words. To the extent that events internal to the organism are important in attaining solution, then conceptual behavior is *in part* verbal.

It is not difficult, moreover, to find many so-called studies of verbal learning which obviously involve important conceptual components. A few examples are worth noting. (1) *Cue selection.* Underwood (1963) has reviewed a small but growing set of experiments aimed at exploring the nature of the functional stimulus in verbal paired associates tasks. Underwood notes that, under some circumstances, subjects will associate the required response not with the nominal stimulus (that is, that presented by the experimenter) but with some portion of it. When the stimuli are nonsense syllables the subject may attend only to their initial letters. If each is different then the first letter alone is sufficient to cue the proper response. Using a fraction of the available stimulus may simplify the task without interfering with the requisite behaviors. To the extent that this selective process occurs, the subject is abstracting a relevant cue or set of cues—a characteristic which we readily recognize as an important component of conceptual behavior. (2) *Clustering.* Bousfield (1953) and others have used the method of free learning and recall to investigate what amounts to a grouping phenomenon in verbal learning. The subject is allowed first to study a list of words and is then required to recall as many of them as possible within a fixed time interval. No constraints are placed on the order of item recall. If there exist certain words in the original list which are members of or are related to the same generic category, such as *animal* names or names of *professions*, these items are often recalled together in a sequence, regardless of their positions in the original list. This organizing tendency in the recall process is called clustering and is clearly a manifestation of the utilization of previously learned concepts or item groupings. (3) *Learning grammatical rules.* In the last ten years a vigorous research effort aimed at an understanding of how grammatical rules are acquired and used has begun. Several current comprehensive summaries of progress are available (for example, Brown and Fraser, 1963). It is clear that this work is not only similar to but also contains important implications for the study of conceptual rule learning.

It is patently impossible to review in these pages all research problems which span verbal and conceptual behavior. Nor is such a review crucial to our general purposes. This section concentrates on a highly selected literature, describing studies wherein either or both the stimulus materials and the requisite response system have important verbal components. In most cases the tasks used require the subject to categorize meaningful words rather than physical objects or their pictorial representations. In general, the classifications arise from word meanings rather than any physical characteristics. Very often the words which are positive instances of a given category have only a single meaning in common, thus resembling the unidimensional concept in our original system of definitions. In all cases the accent is on the effects of manipulable verbal characteristics of the situation on performance in conceptual tasks.

The research considered is presented in two parts. The first is concerned directly with characteristics of verbal associations and their effects on concept learning. The second centers on some studies of verbal concepts wherein variables similar to those known to have reliable effects on performance in nonverbal problems (for example, number of positive and negative instances) are explored.

Dominance of Concepts

When any verbal stimulus is presented to a subject, it may elicit one or more of a number of verbal response associates. For example, "snow" may suggest "white," "cold," "rain," "winter," etc. Further, the specific associates of a given stimulus may vary appreciably among individuals. Any subject may be said to have a hierarchy of associates for each of many stimuli, and within any single hierarchy the strengths of associates may take on different values.

In many verbal concept-learning tasks the subject is required to discover a way of grouping or classifying names of common, concrete objects. The names are the stimuli, the counterparts of geometric designs, or other physical entities in most of the studies discussed earlier. Generally, the basis for classifying together a set of different names is some single associate which is common to all of them. For example, "snow," "tooth," "chalk," and "milk" all suggest "white" and may be grouped accordingly. One might imagine that such a grouping would be learned or discovered rapidly because the common descriptive response is associated strongly with each of these names. But another set of items, say, "bone," "collar," "frost," and "lint," to which "white" is also an associate, would probably take longer to learn because of their considerably weaker associations with the common response. The variable we are dealing with, that is, relative strength of associations between a name and a descriptive response, is called response *dominance*.

Underwood and Richardson (1956a) calibrated dominance for a restricted set of names. Their study was limited to a particular type of descriptive associate for names—sense impressions. Specifically, they presented 213 common nouns, one at a time, to 153 college students who were instructed to give as an associate to each the first sensory impression (for example, "large," "circular," "red," "strong") which came to mind. The associates of each word were subsequently analyzed to determine the percentage of subjects who produced the same (or similar) associate for each noun. As an example, to the word "cigar" 40% of subjects responded with "smelly," 26% with "brown," and 14% with "long." Dominance is defined in terms of the percentages, so that in the example "smelly" is the most dominant response and "long" the least (of those given) to "cigar." As we have seen, different nouns will, with varying frequencies, elicit the same sense impression. Thus, for purposes of learning tasks one can construct sets of nouns which represent the same concept (sense impression) so as to control or vary dominance level systematically. Some illustrative materials from the Underwood-Richardson study appear in Table 2.

Table 2

Illustrative material from the Underwood-Richardson (1956a) calibration

Stimulus Word	Associates					
	Word	%	Word	%	Word	%
Anchor	Heavy	57	Metallic	15	Hard	7
Badge	Shiny	32	Metallic	27	Round	21
Cabin	Small	39	Woody	28	Brown	11
Diamond	Shiny	65	Hard	15	Clear	9
Eye	Round	32	Small	10	Brown	8
Forest	Green	52	Dark	14	Big	12
Ginger	Strong	40	Brown	15	Sweet	11
Head	Round	66	Hard	9	Small	5
Ivory	White	65	Hard	14	Smooth	12
Jellyfish	Slimy	49	Soft	31	Small	5
Kitten	Soft	41	Small	25	Hairy	13
Linen	White	59	Soft	14	Smooth	9
Moss	Green	52	Soft	22	Wet	6
Needle	Sharp	53	Pointed	15	Small	9
Onion	Smelly	49	White	15	Strong	14
Paste	Sticky	64	White	16	Slimy	7
Rice	White	54	Small	24	Hard	6
Sheep	Fuzzy	49	White	23	Soft	14
Teeth	White	72	Sharp	8	Hard	5
Waist	Small	43	Round	24	Narrow	12
Zoo	Big	32	Smelly	30	Noisy	7

Column one presents the stimulus nouns given to each subject. The remaining columns show the three most frequent (most dominant) responses, along with the percentages of subjects making them. It should be noted that some stimulus words, not appearing in this tabulation, elicited fewer than three distinctly different responses.

In an experiment using these calibrated materials, Underwood and Richardson (1956b) explored the obvious question of a relationship between dominance and speed of learning. They made up lists of 24 nouns, of which 4 were instances of each of six concepts. The subject was told that there were six sets of 4 related nouns in the list and that each noun within a set could be described by the same word. He was to guess the correct response for each noun as the list of items was presented serially. The experimenter indicated whether the guess was right or wrong immediately after it was given. The list was presented 20 times, with the order of words varied on each trial. If the subject learned all groupings within the trial series, he responded with only 6 different words since each response was correct for 4 different noun stimuli. Of the six different concepts in a list, two were high, two were medium, and two were low in dominance level. High-dominance concepts consisted of noun-associate relationships averaging about 75% in the norms. In other words, the nouns used to illustrate a concept at this level all elicited the same associate from about 75% of people. Similarly, concepts of medium and low dominance averaged approximately 41% and 16% respectively.

The results were not unexpected. The higher the dominance level, the greater the number of concepts learned, and the greater the number of correct responses given. Further, the higher the dominance level, the fewer the competing or interfering responses; that is, associates of a given noun which were incorrect in the context of the particular concepts to be learned. The data clearly established dominance as a significant variable in verbal concept learning. The basis of its import no doubt lies in the fact that dominance is a rather direct measure of the strength of preestablished conceptual relationships. Whereas high-dominance concepts may need only to be recognized by subjects, low-dominance associations probably require a greater amount of search and strengthening before they become suitably functional.

In the traditional paired-associates technique used by Underwood and Richardson it is difficult to be certain that all subjects learned the concepts (particularly the low-dominant ones) embodied in a list as opposed to merely memorizing the individual pairs. Noting this problem, Coleman (1964) set out to replicate and extend the Underwood-Richardson results with a procedure less subject to rote-memorization effects. In this experiment the subject was presented simultaneously with 4 nouns and was required to produce a single adjective which described them all. Thirty-two problems of this nature were constructed, half of them containing nouns of a high-dominant concept and half with nouns of a low-dominant concept. High dominance concepts (9.4 seconds) were solved significantly more rapidly on the average than low dominance (15.8 seconds). Thus these data are quite compatible with the earlier findings, and we may conclude that more than a simple difference in amount of required rote memorization contributes to the dominance effect.

DOMINANCE RANK. Some nouns suggest many associates (concepts) while others suggest few. As a result, in the Underwood-Richardson norms one can find items for which the dominance value of the most frequent concept is 90% or above, indicating high agreement among subjects, and others for which the most dominant concept has a value of 20% or less. There are then two characteristics of dominance which may contribute to its over-all effect; one is the absolute dominance value, expressed in percentages, and the other is the rank of the concept in the set of associates given to the noun in question. An example may clarify the distinction. To the noun "belly," the associate "round" has Rank 1 (the most frequently given associate) and a dominance value of 43%. The associate "soft" has Rank 2 and a dominance value of 24%. For the noun "pail," "metallic" has Rank 1 and a dominance value of 24%. Thus "metallic" - "pail" and "soft" - "belly" are equal in dominance value but different in dominance rank according to the Underwood-Richardson norms.

Mednick and Halpern (1962) explored the rank variable in an experimental task patterned after that of Underwood and Richardson on the hypothesis that performance would improve directly with concept rank. Each list learned by a subject contained one group of 4 nouns belonging to a concept of Rank 1 and a second group belonging to a concept of Rank 2, the mean dominance value of concepts being held constant. Concepts having the higher rank position were learned in fewer trials and with fewer errors, thus demonstrating the importance of rank in determining the previously described dominance effect. It is not clear from these results, however, how much of the over-all effect should be attributed to rank and how much to absolute dominance value. A crucial study which remains to be conducted is one wherein both dominance rank and value are varied within the same experimental design and task. The outcome of this investigation would provide a clearer picture of the role of dominance in verbal concept learning.

DOMINANCE VARIABILITY. In most studies the mean dominance of instances has been systematically varied, while the variance of dominance values (differences among instances of the same concept) has been small and held relatively constant across concepts. There is some reason to believe that dominance variability may also be a significant determiner of performance. If, for example, we include in a given set of instances of a concept one noun with very high dominance it may elicit the correct associate (concept) early in the training trials. This in turn may, by simple contiguity, make the relationship of low-dominant instances within the set to the same associate more obvious and thereby speed up the required learning. On these grounds one may expect more rapid learning of a high-variance concept relative to a low-variance (all instances of roughly equal dominance) concept, even though the average dominance level of the members of both concepts is the same.

This proposition was tested in an experiment conducted by Freedman and Mednick (1958). Subjects learned lists of 12 nouns—four instances of each of three concepts. The lists contained concepts of equal (and relatively low) mean dominance level (24%) but different variances. The low-variance concepts were represented by instances with homogeneous dominance values while any high-variance set contained one instance of exceptionally high dominance. To illustrate, the concept "small" may be embodied in a list with either high or low variance. For low variance the following instances (and their values) could be used: "cradle" (24%), "closet" (24%), "rice" (24%), and "pin" (22%). For high variance "gnat" (76%), "needle" (9%), "stone" (7%), and "canary" (5%) are suitable. Note that both sets have the same average dominance. In accord with expectations high-variance concepts were learned more quickly and with fewer errors than low-variance concepts. To determine the correctness of an assumption that the high-variance group was facilitated through an early elicitation of the correct concept name by its most dominant instance, the average trial on which the first correct response occurred was computed. The resulting value was 4 for high-variance and 10 for low-variance concepts, thus supporting one hypothesis on the operational effect of dominance variability. Apparently the high dominant instance brings out the correct response early, allowing contiguity then to establish its connection with other instances within the same grouping.

A WEAKNESS OF THE UNDERWOOD-RICHARDSON TECHNIQUE. While the normative materials of Underwood and Richardson (1956a) are adequate for many experimental purposes, their procedure suffers the important disadvantage of being based on extralaboratory experience over which the experimenter has no control. This creates problems for rigorous experiments. For one thing, a dominance value is a "group" norm which may not reflect the actual degree of association between noun and concept for any particular individual. The dominance values reported in the foregoing experiments are certainly not the same for all subjects. Further, the Underwood-Richardson calibration was based on just one type of conceptual relation among items— common sensory associates. Though "suit" and "dress" may not suggest the same sensory impressions, they are no doubt related through other conceptual or associative systems. Such unaccounted-for relations among nouns in the Underwood-Richardson lists probably introduce an appreciable amount of "noise" or indeterminate variability into experimental data.

Granting the existence of these problems, a question arises about possible procedures for circumventing or eliminating them. One such procedure has been advanced by Thysell and Schulz (1964). Their technique requires subjects to learn a prescribed pattern of associations for initially "meaningless" verbal items, such as "menad," under controlled laboratory conditions. To test the feasibility of developing significant dominance values (or associative strengths), the following routine was used. First, subjects were given paired-associates training with nine nonsense items assigned in sets of three to three adjectival responses. The length of this training was 10, 20, or 40 trials for different groups of subjects, length of training serving as an operational definition of associative strength or dominance. In the concept problem, subjects were required to discover the correct method of sorting the nonsense items into three groups. For the relevant-associates group the basis of sorting was the existence of a common associate. That is, all items paired during initial learning with the same sense impression were to be sorted together. The items were similarly sorted into three categories by the remaining subjects; however, the prior paired-associates training of these subjects was irrelevant and provided no useful guide for sorting.

Sorting performance improved directly with number of paired-associates trials when this training involved the sensory impressions which were relevant in the conceptual task. Precisely the opposite effect was found when dominance of irrelevant associates was increased through prior training. Thus, Thysell and Schulz concluded that it is feasible to study dominance effects in verbal concept learning using artificial stimulus units whose associations are developed in the laboratory. The technique offers some promise of bypassing the above-mentioned difficulties arising from the use of normative materials in that the associations are known and may be controlled and/or manipulated experimentally for the individual subject.

Other Variables

Many factors enter to determine qualitative and quantitative aspects of conceptual behavior in nonverbal problems. There has been a limited amount of work on essentially the same variables in verbal problems. While it is only common sense to expect parallel results, it is instructive to consider some of these studies for the procedures are somewhat different and there are a few unique and interesting findings.

POSITIVE AND NEGATIVE INSTANCES. Mayzner (1962) reported a study of types of instances which adds some useful information to what has been learned in nonverbal experiments. He argued that the numbers of positive and negative verbal instances of a concept should have significant but opposite effects on the speed with which the concept is discovered. This hypothesis was based on the assumption that any word will elicit some one or more associates. The more positive words available, the more likely it is that two (or more) of them will evoke the "correct" associate, that is, the concept, thus leading to solution. Conversely, negative instances should evoke unrelated, presumably competing associates thereby slowing down the process of discovery. In a test of this proposition, subjects were given problems wherein a set of words was displayed, each being identified as positive or negative by the experimenter. The subject then was required (a) to pick out the one item among the negative instances which actually belonged in the positive class and (b) to state his reason for the selection; that is, to name the concept. Four such problems were given to each subject and the time taken to solve each was recorded. There were 12 conditions determined by forming all combinations of problems with 2, 3, 4, or 5 positive instances and 2, 4, or 6 negative instances.

As the number of positive instances increased, time to solution decreased significantly; further, there was a small inhibitory effect resulting from an increase in number of negative instances. The data are similar to and consistent with the previously cited experiments by (a) Hovland and Weiss (1953) who demonstrated the relative greater importance of positive as compared to negative instances and (b) Bourne et al. (1964) who showed that an increase in the number of available instances facilitated conceptual performance. They suggest that subjects rely only slightly, if at all, on negative information in an attempt to form or identify a concept. Thus, the evocation of irrelevant associates by negative instances has only a minor inhibiting effect on performance.

Mayzner's study employed only one of many possible arrangements of positive and negative instances in verbal problems. If, for example, he had varied the dominance of positive and negative instances, some more important effects may have appeared. Relevant to this question is a study performed by Kendler and Karasik (1958). Using much the same technique as Mayzner, these experimenters presented subjects with eight nouns, four positive and four negative instances of a concept to be discovered. One positive instance was identified by the experimenter whereupon the subject was asked to pick out the three other positive instances from the seven remaining nouns and tell why or how they were related. The positive instances in all problems had moderate dominance values (approximately 45%), while the negative instances, which in two experimental conditions were all exemplars of another concept, had either high (greater than 65%) or low (less than 28%) dominance. In a third condition the negative instances were unrelated to one another, each having a high dominance relation with a different concept. Kendler and Karasik found that concepts were more readily discovered and named if the negative instances were all members of the same concept and dominantly related to it. Their interpretation of this result assumes that concept identification involves (a) learning a common (implicit, mediational) response to a set of different objects or words and (b) learning different and distinctive responses to items outside the concept (negative instances). As such, concept identification depends on implicit (or explicit) response differentiation for the two types of items. If the words which are irrelevant to the concept to be discovered have ready-made, strong tendencies to evoke implicit responses that are different from that which is common to the relevant words, attainment of problem solution is facilitated.

NUMBER OF IRRELEVANT "DIMENSIONS." Typically, the objects or stimulus patterns which are instances of a given concept have characteristics or attributes in common with the instances of other different concepts. Because these overlapping attributes and the dimensions they represent cannot be used to distinguish between the concepts they have been labeled irrelevant. We have seen several examples of the inhibiting effects of irrelevant features on the identification of nonverbal concepts. Geometric designs represent a useful type of stimulus material for the study of irrelevant (and relevant) attributes because they are readily dimensionalized along obvious and familiar lines, such as color, form, and so on. However, verbal instances and verbal concepts have irrelevant attributes also. Any word, representative of one concept, may have descriptive characteristics in common with exemplars of a different concept. Suppose that "tomato," "baseball," and "collar" are used in a list of words to illustrate the concept "round" and that the list also contains words which exemplify the concepts "red," "hard," and "white." Here "tomato," an instance of "round," has a characteristic associate in common with the instances of "red." Likewise, "baseball" and "collar" overlap on irrelevant dimensions with instances of "hard" and "white." While the analogy of irrelevant dimensions between verbal and nonverbal lists is not direct and while it is difficult to be as certain about the nature and extent of irrelevant overlap in verbal concepts, still it seems reasonable to draw the generalization from nonverbal studies that irrelevant and overlapping attributes among concepts in the same list will retard performance. Indeed, the greater the number of overlapping associates, the slower learning should be.

Underwood (1957) tested this hypothesis. He constructed three lists, each containing four instances (nouns) of four different concepts. The lists differed in terms of the amount of overlap in associates among instances of the different concepts. In List O no instance of one concept had any common associate with instances of any other concept. In List 1 all instances had exactly one common associate with instances of a different concept. In List 2 instances had an average of 1.9 overlapping associates with other concepts. (As an example from List 2, "rice," used as an instance of the concept "small," also suggests both "white" and "hard" which were two other concepts embodied in the same list.) Subjects were to learn the "correct" concept (or response) for each noun by the standard reception procedure for verbal materials. Parallel to experiments on nonverbal concepts, learning was retarded by the existence of cross-concept associates or irrelevant attributes. However, while List 1 and 2 were both harder to learn than List O, there was no difference in performance on the former two. This observation is clearly discrepant from findings with nonverbal concepts where number of irrelevant dimensions has been shown to be an important source of interference up through at least five dimensions (Archer, Bourne, and Brown, 1954). Whether this comparison is indicative of some real difference between verbal and nonverbal concepts or merely an artifact of the insensitivity of normative data (Underwood and Richardson, 1956a) to all the associative overlap among nouns is difficult to say. Further experiments perhaps employing the laboratory procedure of Thysell and Schulz (1964) for establishing (relevant and irrelevant) associates for verbal items would yield more definitive evidence on this question.

SUCCESSIVE VERSUS SIMULTANEOUS PRESENTATION. Crouse and Duncan (1963) performed an experiment involving both dominance and method of stimulus presentation as variables. The subject was instructed to sort a group of nouns into four categories on the basis of the sensory impression each evoked. Each category was "labeled" by three sample nouns belonging to that concept. The test nouns were to be placed into the category whose samples suggested the same impression or concept. For different subjects the samples were of high (90%) or low (50%) dominance. For half the subjects within each sample-dominance condition the nouns to be sorted were either high or low in dominance. Finally, the four groups so-treated were further subdivided so that half sorted the nouns as they were presented by the experimenter one at a time, while the others were shown all the nouns to be sorted and thus were allowed to make comparisons among them.

All three variables had significant effects. High sample-dominance and high instance-dominance both facilitated performance. These results are to be expected on the basis of the preceding experiments, even though the conceptual task was different. Consistent with the results of nonverbal studies, simultaneous presentation produced fewer errors and more correct responses than successive presentation of instances. In the present case this is very likely a consequence of what may be called a "priming" effect. That is, the simultaneous evocation of the same or similar associates from two or more available (visible) nouns probably increases the strength of the associate and the likelihood of the same response being elicited by other words belonging to the same category. These data suggest again the continuity of results across experiments on verbal and nonverbal concepts.

CONTIGUITY OF INSTANCES. There have been several tests, with positive outcome, of Underwood's (1952) hypothesis about the importance of temporal contiguity among instances of a given concept (for example, Kurtz and Hovland, 1956). Schulz, Miller, and Radtke (1963) performed the parallel experiment with verbal materials. Lists of 24 nouns, 4 belonging to each of six concepts, were prepared. Three different levels of concept dominance, namely, high (75%), medium (41%), and low (16%) were represented within each list. In cases of high contiguity all four instances of the same concept were presented successively on each learning trial. For medium contiguity two of the four instances of a given concept were presented successively within the list, while one or more instances of another concept were interpolated before the remaining two instances occurred. Under low contiguity no two instances of a given concept at any time appeared successively.

Results were in complete accord with expectations based on Underwood's position. As shown in Figure 14, both increasing dominance and increasing contiguity had reliable facilitory effects on learning the appropriate conceptual groupings of nouns. The findings with respect to contiguity are particularly interesting, for they establish an extension and further generality for Underwood's theoretical orientation across a wide range of procedural conditions and stimulus materials.

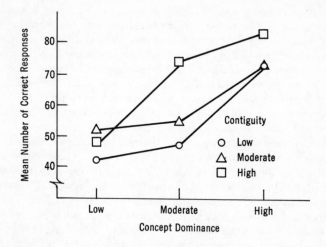

Figure 14. Performance in verbal concept tasks as a function of dominance and contiguity among concept instances. Data from Schulz, Miller, and Radtke (1963).

VERBAL LABELS FOR NONVERBAL STIMULUS ATTRIBUTES. When nonverbal stimulus materials are used in concept-learning experiments, they are generally quite familiar, common objects. Despite their nonverbal nature the attributes of these objects usually have well-known, easily produced labels. Indeed, it is often argued that mediational activities involved in arriving at the solution of a conceptual problem are in large measure verbal, which of course implies use of labels by subjects and thus some sort of translation of physical representations into words. If the intermediate verbal activity is necessary or even helpful in solving conceptual problems, one would expect that stimuli with familiar labels would be classifiable more easily and more rapidly than stimuli lacking such labels. Further, of two sets of unfamiliar stimuli, those on which the subject has been given some degree of pretraining designed to provide verbal labels should be easier to use.

To study these hypotheses, Rasmussen and Archer (1961) constructed a set of nonsense figures which bore no obvious similarity to any common shape or object. Some of the figures were 8-sided and others were 10-sided.

In addition, the figures varied in color, size, and several other dimensions. During pretraining, prior to a conceptual problem in which these stimuli were to be categorized, subjects learned distinctive verbal labels for the 8- and 10-sided figures. Performance was significantly better on subsequent conceptual tasks with shape (sidedness) as a relevant rather than an irrelevant dimension. From this the authors concluded that available verbal labels enter into and contribute to stimulus discrimination and mediation processes which are fundamental to problem solving. Verbal pretraining produced more rapid solutions when shape was a relevant rather than an irrelevant dimension in the concept problem.

Comment

A single theme underlies most of the current research on verbal concepts. The primary aim has been to study much the same variables as have been shown to be important in nonverbal task settings. Indeed, there is little substantial difference either in purpose or results between programs of research on verbal and nonverbal concepts. The main distinction is simply a change in stimulus materials from objects or their pictorial representations to their conventional linguistic symbols. While it is interesting to know that such a change can be made without serious modifications in the principles and functional relationships that govern performance in problematic situations, much deeper questions and issues seem hardly to be touched by current experimentation. For example, we still know very little about the critical verbal components of the behavioral sequence which takes place between the presentation of problem elements and overt performance leading to solution. We have only fragmentary information about the subject's spontaneous translation of the problematic situation into a verbal code. Factual evidence on the degree to which linguistic tools or devices serve the problem solving process is unimpressive.

Research on the interrelation of language and problem solving has barely begun. Resolutions of remaining questions may not come easy or soon. There is no guarantee that they will come at all, using the admittedly primitive research techniques that are presently available. It will take considerable investigative ingenuity and talent if we expect to make significant progress in the near future.

FINAL REMARK

The principal aim of this chapter has been to review some of the empirical work on organismic variables in conceptual behavior. At the outset it was clear that research in the area is sparse, primitive, and unsystematic. While this discussion may have served only to confirm that fact, it is at least reasonable to hope that by describing the technical and substantive problems facing the experimenter we have also presented a challenge. It is not possible to provide a simple over-all statement which summarizes our present knowledge. There are too many gaps and too many loose ends. Rather, it seems more reasonable at this point to invite wider participation in achieving the empirical results which will contribute to a better understanding of human variables in conceptual problems.

VI

Concluding Statement

THE AIM OF THE PRECEDING CHAPTERS has been to describe the experimental psychology of conceptual behavior. While we shall not attempt a detailed summary, it is useful to recount some of the topics and problems discussed.

The first three chapters provided an epistemological, technological, and theoretical background for current research. In Chapter I an effort was made (*a*) to present "the concept of a concept" from the point of view of experimental psychology and to contrast it with the informal notions of a layman, (*b*) to develop a simple and limited yet workable set of definitions for the structural and behavioral elements of a conceptual problem, and (*c*) to outline in general form the two experimental paradigms which have served most empirical work. Chapter II presented a formal analysis of concepts and conceptual behavior. It made the critical distinction between defining or relevant stimulus *attributes* of a concept and *rules* which determine the function of these attributes in dividing the domain of stimulus objects to which the concept properly applies. Further, it specified some components of behavior which are identified with learning about and using attributes and rules in conceptual problems. Finally, it supplied a preview of the intimate relationship between language and concepts. Some of the more important theoretical issues were discussed in Chapter III. It was noted first that two main themes persist throughout the history of psychology's attempt to interpret and explain conceptual processes. On the one hand are S-R theories which portray concept formation as a gradual "stamping-in" of associations between stimulus attributes and classificatory responses. The major competing position views the learner as an active hypothesis tester who solves a conceptual problem by generating, testing, and rejecting plausible solutions until he finds one that works. A possible rapprochement of these two traditions exists in what has been called the mediated or multistage S-R interpretation which makes allowances for the existence of hypotheses in the form of previously learned, internalized response-sequences and associations.

121

Having established a rationale and technique acceptable to experimental psychology, we proceeded in the next two chapters to survey the most recent empirical work. The research discussed provides not only the basis for our current understanding of conceptual behavior but also the data by which we may judge the adequacy of unifying theoretical systems. While the classification of experiments is essentially arbitrary, Chapter IV provided coverage of the effects of so-called task conditions; that is, response, stimulus, informative feedback, timing variables, and the type of conceptual rule. Chapter V consisted of a review of research on processes and variables which are related to the organism; that is, memory, motivation, intelligence, perception, transfer of training, and the learning of verbal concepts. Despite the fact that experimental work on conceptual behavior is a relatively recent development, considerable detailed information is already available. Indeed, the coverage of Chapters IV and V falls far short of being exhaustive. It seems, however, that the research is not in all cases systematic. While knowledge about organismic variables is especially fragmentary, we were able to note some issues in need of clarification under almost every heading. The interested student will surely find no shortage of important problems to explore.

SOME NOTABLE LIMITATIONS ON THIS SURVEY

Certain problems and questions received little or no consideration in this review. Decisions about what to cover were based on several criteria not the least important of which were (a) the problem's accessibility to experimental techniques, (b) the availability of a reasonable amount of empirically based knowledge, and (c) the degree of relevance to human behavior. Nonetheless, the omission or scanty treatment of certain topics must be viewed as a serious limitation. As a way of recognizing their importance and of showing their place in the over-all picture of conceptual processes, we briefly note in the following section four of the major problems which have been neglected.

A Comparative Psychology of Conceptual Behavior

What are the abilities of animals, lower than man, to learn and to use concepts? This is a question well-worth exploring for the techniques of comparative or cross-species investigations have contributed immeasurably to the scientific knowledge and understanding of many behavioral processes. The results of comparative studies can supply information not only about the characteristics and limitations of a particular species of animal but also on possible systematic phylogenetic changes in the structure of behavior which may help us to understand the activities of man.

While some writers doubt the ability of inarticulate organisms to form true concepts (Osgood, 1954; Hunt, 1962), the existence of a strict discontinuity between man and lower animal forms on this behavioral dimension has not been satisfactorily demonstrated. In fact, the empirical evidence is such as to suggest that some species other than man operate on a fairly high conceptual level (Kendler, 1961). The technique of comparative research which is most clearly related to concept learning as it is studied in human beings is that of learning set studies. We have noted earlier Harlow's (1959) position with respect to conceptual behavior and its relationship to the learning set phenomenon. Such a procedure has been extensively used to explore the performance of various animals, such as cats, raccoons, and monkeys, in problem series which require consistent responding to common features, such as object quality or object oddity, of otherwise different stimuli. The adaptability of the learning set paradigm to various species of organisms and its apparent sensitivity to phylogenetic and neurophysiological differences among animals has led Harlow and others to propose its use as a general test of intellectual capacity.

Another example of the value of a comparative approach is contained in the work of Kendler and Kendler (1962) on solution shifts. In this we find evidence for important changes in the properties of conceptual and problem-solving behavior, both internal and overt, as we ascend the phylogenetic scale from rat to man.

Except for brief glimpses the study of conceptual behavior in lower animals—important as it may be—has been given little attention in this review. Our primary concern has been man, in whom the relevant abilities are maximal. However, it seems clear that further exploration of the performance of lower animals in comparable or related problematic situations will yield a clearer, better integrated picture of these behavioral processes than is currently available.

A Developmental Psychology of Conceptual Behavior

Another line of research, for which the treatment has been minimal, is the study of developmental changes in behavior. Experiments designed to explore performance of human beings at various levels or stages of growth hold great promise of supplying critical information on the evolution of complex cognitive or mental abilities and of a more complete understanding of adult behavior.

Research of an *experimental* nature on this problem is a surprisingly recent undertaking, and as a consequence, the available evidence is quite fragmentary, precluding the statement of strong or general conclusions (Fowler, 1962). The empirical work, as Kendler (1961) has pointed out, arises largely from three sources. One is the prodigious effort of Piaget and collaborators (e.g., Inhelder and Piaget, 1958) who, on the basis of seminaturalistic observations of the behavior of children in a variety of problematic situations, have produced a broad and sophisticated, though provocative and controversial, theory of the intellectual development. Few would question the interest value and excitement of Piaget's findings and interpretations. But in part because of the relative looseness of his methods, the obscurity (until recently) of much of his work, and the difficulty of his style and a consequent lack of understanding by many psychologists, Piaget's contribution has to date made no great impact on the experimental approach to conceptual behavior. Still, we note with enthusiasm some indications of quite definite influence by Piaget on current research (for example, Bruner, 1964; Kooistra, 1964; King, 1964). While it is difficult at present to evaluate the significance of this trend, it holds some definite promise of important insights into complex human behavior.

A second impetus to research on developmental processes comes from a general concern with symbolic or mediational processes, particularly verbal, and their control of overt actions (Reese, 1962). One systematic position (Luria, 1957; Kendler and Kendler, 1962) has it that, as the human child grows older, his self-generated, implicit behavior comes gradually to mediate and to regulate his overt behavior. The pattern of this growth or maturational sequence and its determination of conceptual activities have been the subject of a number of enlightening experiments, some of which have been reported earlier. Further empirical clarification is needed, and fortunately considerable research is presently in progress.

The final approach taken in many recent developmental studies uses the methodology of learning set formation. As with cross-species comparisons, this procedural device has been shown to be quite sensitive to changes in chronological age, and intellectual capacity. It has the interesting further advantage of being relatively species-free in the sense that it can be adapted to the study of developmental factors in various organisms. Thus, systematic experimentation on the formation of learning sets should contribute in due measure to our knowledge of age changes in intellectual and conceptual functioning.

Pathology in Thinking and Conceptual Behavior

Nearly all experimental studies of conceptual processes have been undertaken with the aim of understanding "normal" behavior. The implicit assumption seems to be that, when we know how the typical human being behaves, we shall be in better position to study and to explain aberrations in thinking. However, interest in pathological thought has a long history in psychology, and there is a considerable literature plus a substantial amount of current research on this problem.

Most of the available studies are better described as clinical rather than experimental in technique. Their aim, generally, has been to compare qualitatively the performance of individuals diagnosed as belonging to one or another psychiatric category or as suffering some organic, usually neurological, deficit with the performance of normal subjects on the same conceptual problem or task. There is the classic work of Vigotsky (1934) who argued that the very essence of schizophrenia is a loss of ability to think in terms of abstract concepts and a regression to a more primitive concrete level similar to that on which children operate. Later elaborations on this approach indicate specifiable, if bizarre, characteristics of the concepts formed and used by schizophrenics and their pervasive tendency to overgeneralize and to violate normal concept boundaries (Epstein, 1953; Chapman and Taylor, 1957). There is further some important evidence implicating motivational (Cavanaugh, 1958) and personality (Fey, 1954) variables in the performance of schizophrenics on conceptual problems. Parallel studies have been conducted with other classes of functional disorder; for example, the neuroses.

Interest in organic disturbances in conceptual behavior stems largely from the work of Goldstein (1940; also Goldstein and Scheerer, 1941) with brain-injured war veterans. While his opinions on the effects of neurological damage, particularly massive destructions of the frontal lobes, on human personality and behavior are speculative, they provided both the stimulus and the guidance for clinical explorations of the relevant problems. In brief, Goldstein described the effects of brain damage as a primitivization of thought. He viewed this type of patient as suffering from a boundedness or rigidity in thinking. Whereas the normal person can operate either on a concrete or an abstract level of conception and organization, the brain-damaged person, like the schizophrenic, has lost his capacity for dealing with abstract concepts. Goldstein and his co-workers devised various clinical tests of conceptual functioning for the diagnosis and characterization of brain-injured and functionally disturbed patients. These tools, and their later refinements (for example, Halstead, 1947) have also served important functions in some more experimentally oriented programs of research (for example, Shure and Halstead, 1958; Doehring and Reitan, 1961), which have investigated, among other issues, location and extent of injury as factors in behavioral deficit. Fairly complete reviews of the literature pertaining to the effects of brain lesions (Klebanoff, Singer, and Wilensky, 1954; Milner, 1954) and of organic deterioration with age (Inglis, 1958) on intellectual functions are available to the interested reader.

Social Variables

In real life the concepts that human beings form and use apply to objects and events of motivational and functional significance. Furthermore, the process of forming concepts is typically not a solitary affair but occurs in the course of social interaction with others. There are, then, questions of obvious major importance pertaining to the role of "social" variables in conceptual behavior.

One illustrative problem of considerable significance centers on the learning, functioning, and change of attitudes and prejudices. Some experts in the area consider the laboratory methods and techniques of concept formation to be directly applicable to the problem. Rhine (1958; also Sherif and Sherif, 1956) defined attitudes as a special class of concepts distinguished by their involvement of an evaluative or an affective dimension. Thus, a child may learn to distinguish between Negroes, Orientals, Caucasians, and to classify others whom he meets accordingly on the basis of physical or physiognomic characteristics such as skin color, facial features, and the like. If so we say he has formed a (socially relevant) concept, or more properly a conceptual system since an array of categories is involved. If, in addition, the child experiences some personal unpleasantness with individuals belonging to one (or more) category or is led to believe that a certain class of people is "bad" or "dirty" or "unreliable," then the concept comes to be affect laden and to embody an evaluative dimension along with its physical attributes. As such the concept may be called an attitude or prejudice.

Rhine (1958) developed an experimental method for studying the acquisition and change of attitudes which is based on standard concept-formation techniques. In his procedure the physical stimulus patterns (the positive and negative instances) are replaced by trait names which the subject learns to sort into two categories—either (1) characteristic or (2) not characteristic of some hypothetical, newly discovered tribe of people. Among the several dimensions along which these traits vary is the evaluative one; that is, some traits such as *honest* or *handsome* are generally considered quite desirable in any person while others such as *loud* or *aggressive* are undesirable. To the extent that desirable (undesirable) traits are shown to be characteristic of the tribe, a positive (negative) attitude is said to develop. Rhine and his coworkers reported some experiments using this method in which consistency of assigning positive or negative traits to people (Rhine and Silum, 1958) and the presence or absence of peers (Rhine, 1958) during learning were found to be important variables determining rate of attitude formation and its subsequent resistance to change.

At this writing the psychological inquiry into conceptual behavior can best be described as lively. Convinced by common sense and common observation that most human activity involves learning about and dealing with categories or groups of things rather than with the unique, and by the success of pioneering (albeit relatively recent) research efforts (for example, Bruner, Goodnow, and Austin, 1956; Underwood and Richardson, 1956a, b; Hovland, 1952) that conceptual activity is accessible to experimental investigative procedures, psychologists are at present engaged in a determined empirical and theoretical analysis of the problem. What has been presented in these pages is a survey or cross-section of a field in a state of rapid flux. It is safe to predict that, in the next few years, (a) many of the questions raised by this review will be suitably answered, (b) some of the tentative conclusions we have drawn will become solidified while others will require drastic modification, and (c) our over-all understanding of the problems and processes identified with this area will achieve proper scientific status. This being the case, one may seriously question the wisdom of attempting a review, such as this, on the grounds of prematurity. There is only one reply to this criticism. It has been shown—hopefully—that a body of knowledge (though in some respects scanty) does exist. Its coherent presentation has been the goal. As for the current interest and prolific effort of experimental psychologists engaged in the study of conceptual processes—we would not have it any other way.

References

ADAMS, J. Concepts as operators. *Psychol. Rev.*, 1953, **60**, 241–251.

ADAMS, J. A. Multiple versus single problem training in human problem solving. *J. exp. Psychol.*, 1954, **48**, 15–19.

ANDREW, G., & HARLOW, H. F. Performance of macaque monkeys on a test of the concept of generalized triangularity. *Comp. Psychol. Monogr.*, 1948, **19**, No. 3 (Serial No. 100).

ARCHER, E. J. On verbalizations and concepts. In A. W. Melton (Ed.), *Categories of human learning*. New York: Academic Press, 1964.

ARCHER, E. J., BOURNE, L. E., JR., & BROWN, F. G. Concept identification as a function of irrelevant information and instruction. *J. exp. Psychol.*, 1955, **49**, 153–164.

BARCH, A. M. Prediction of recurrent sequences as related to level of irrelevant cues. *J. exp. Psychol.*, 1961, **61**, 410–416.

BATTIG, W. F., & BOURNE, L. E., JR. Concept identification as a function of irrelevant information and instruction. *J. exp. Psychol.*, 1955, **49**, 153–164.

BAUM, MARIAN. Simple concept learning as a function of intra-list generalization. *J. exp. Psychol.*, 1954, **47**, 89–94.

BOURNE, L. E., JR. Effects of delay of information feedback and task complexity on the identification of concepts. *J. exp. Psychol.*, 1957, **54**, 201–207.

BOURNE, L. E., JR. Long term effects of misinformative feedback on concept identification. *J. exp. Psychol.*, 1963, **65**, 139–147. (a)

BOURNE, L. E., JR. Some factors affecting strategies used in problems of concept formation. *Amer. J. Psychol.*, 1963, **76**, 229–238. (b)

BOURNE, L. E., JR. Hypotheses and hypothesis shifts in classification learning. *J. gen. Psychol.*, 1965, **72**, 251–261.

BOURNE, L. E., JR., & BUNDERSON, C. V. Effects of delay of informative feedback and length of postfeedback interval on concept identification. *J. exp. Psychol.*, 1963, **65**, 1–5.

BOURNE, L. E., JR., GOLDSTEIN, S., & LINK, W. E. Concept learning as a function of availability of previously presented information. *J. exp. Psychol.*, 1964, **67**, 439–448.

BOURNE, L. E., JR., GUY, D. E., DODD, D., & JUSTESEN, D. R. Concept identification: The effects of varying length and informational components of the intertrial interval. *J. exp. Psychol.*, 1965, **69**, 624–629.

128

BOURNE, L. E., JR., & HAYGOOD, R. C. The role of stimulus redundancy in the identification of concepts. *J. exp. Psychol.*, 1959, **58**, 232–238.

BOURNE, L. E., JR., & HAYGOOD, R. C. Supplementary report: Effect of redundant relevant information upon the identification of concepts. *J. exp. Psychol.*, 1961, **61**, 259–260.

BOURNE, L. E., JR., & JENNINGS, P. C. The relationship between contiguity and classification learning. *J. gen. Psychol.*, 1963, **69**, 335–338.

BOURNE, L. E., JR., & PENDLETON, R. B. Concept identification as a function of completeness and probability of information feedback. *J. exp. Psychol.*, 1958, **56**, 413–420.

BOURNE, L. E., JR., & RESTLE, F. Mathematical theory of concept identification. *Psychol. Rev.*, 1959, **66**, 278–296.

BOUSFIELD, W. A. The occurrence of clustering in the recall of randomly arranged associates. *J. gen. Psychol.*, 1953, **49**, 229–240.

BOWER, G., & TRABASSO, T. Reversals prior to solution in concept identification. *J. exp. Psychol.*, 1963, **66**, 409–418.

BRALEY, L. S. Some conditions influencing the acquisition and utilization of cues. *J. exp. Psychol.*, 1962, **64**, 62–66.

BROWN, F. G., & ARCHER, E. J. Concept identification as a function of task complexity and distribution of practice. *J. exp. Psychol.*, 1956, **52**, 316–321.

BROWN, R. W., & FRASER, C. The acquisition of syntax. In C. N. Cofer and Barbara S. Musgrave (Eds.), *Verbal behavior and learning.* New York: McGraw-Hill, 1963.

BROWN, R. W., & LENNEBERG, E. H. A study of language and cognition. *J. abnorm. soc. Psychol.*, 1954, **49**, 454–462.

BRUNER, J. S. The course of cognitive growth. *Amer. Psychologist*, 1964, **19**, 1–15.

BRUNER, J. S., GOODNOW, JACQUELINE J., & AUSTIN, G. A. *A study of thinking.* New York: Wiley, 1956.

BRUNER, J. S., WALLACH, M. A., & GALANTER, E. H. The identification of recurrent regularity. *Amer. J. Psychol.*, 1959, **72**, 200–209.

BRUNSWIK, E. *The conceptual framework of psychology.* Internl. Encycl. 1, No. 10. Chicago: The University of Chicago Press, 1952.

BULGARELLA, ROSARIA, & ARCHER, E. J. Concept identification of auditory stimuli as a function of amount of relevant and irrelevant information. *J. exp. Psychol.*, 1962, **63**, 254–257.

BUSS, A. H. Rigidity as a function of reversal and nonreversal shifts in the learning of successive discriminations. *J. exp. Psychol.*, 1953, **45**, 75–81.

BUSS, A. H., & BUSS, EDITH H. The effect of verbal reinforcement combinations on conceptual learning. *J. exp. Psychol.*, 1956, **52**, 282–287.

BYERS, J. L. Strategies and learning set in concept attainment. *Psychol. Rep.*, 1963, **12**, 623–634.

CAHILL, H. E., & HOVLAND, C. I. The role of memory in the acquisition of concepts. *J. exp. Psychol.*, 1960, **59**, 137–144.

CALLANTINE, M. R., & WARREN, J. M. Learning sets in human concept formation. *Psychol. Rep.*, 1955, **1**, 363–367.

CAVANAUGH, D. K. Improvement in the performance of schizophrenics on concept formation tasks as a function of motivational change. *J. abnorm. soc. Psychol.*, 1958, **57**, 8–11.

CHAPMAN, L. J., & TAYLOR, JANET A. Breadth of deviate concepts used by schizophrenics. *J. abnorm. soc. Psychol.*, 1957, **54**, 118–123.

COLEMAN, E. B. Verbal concept learning as a function of instructions and dominance level. *J. exp. Psychol.*, 1964, **68**, 213–214.

CONANT, M. B., & TRABASSO, T. Conjunctive and disjunctive concept formation under equal-information conditions. *J. exp. Psychol.*, 1964, **67**, 250–255.

CROUSE, J. H., & DUNCAN, C. P. Verbal concept sorting as a function of response dominance and sorting method. *J. verb. Learn. verb. Behav.*, 1963, **2**, 480–484.

DE RIVERA, J. Some conditions governing the use of the cue-producing response as an explanatory device. *J. exp. Psychol.*, 1959, **57**, 299–304.

DOEHRING, D. G., & REITAN, R. M. Concept attainment of human adults with lateralized cerebral lesions. *Percept. Mot. Skills*, 1962, **14**, 27–33.

ENGEN, T. Effect of practice and instruction on olfactory thresholds. *Percept. Mot. Skills*, 1960, **10**, 195–198.

EPSTEIN, S. Over-inclusive thinking in a schizophrenic and a control group. *J. consult. Psychol.*, 1953, **17**, 384–388.

FEY, ELIZABETH. The performance of young schizophrenics and young normals on the Wisconsin Card Sorting Test. *J. consult. Psychol.*, 1951, **15**, 311–319.

FOWLER, W. Cognitive learning in infancy and early childhood. *Psychol. Bull.*, 1962, **59**, 116–152.

FREEDMAN, J. L., & MEDNICK, S. A. Ease of attainment of concepts as a function of response dominance variance. *J. exp. Psychol.*, 1958, **55**, 463–466.

FREIBERGS, VAIRA, & TULVING, E. The effect of practice on utilization of information from positive and negative instances in concept identification. *Canad. J. Psychol.*, 1961, **15**, 101–106.

GARNER, W. R. *Uncertainty and structure as psychological concepts.* New York: Wiley, 1962.

GELFAND, S. Effects of prior associations and task complexity upon the identification of concepts. *Psychol. Rep.*, 1958, **4**, 567–574.

GIBSON, ELEANOR J. A systematic application of the concepts of generalization and differentiation to verbal learning. *Psychol. Rev.*, 1940, **47**, 196–229.

GIBSON, ELEANOR J. Perceptual learning. *Annu. Rev. Psychol.*, 1963, **14**, 29–56.

GOLDSTEIN, K. *Human nature in the light of psycho-pathology.* Cambridge, Mass.: Harvard University Press, 1940.

GOLDSTEIN, K., & SCHEERER, M. Abstract and concrete behavior: An experimental study with special tests. *Psychol. Monogr.*, 1941, **53**, No. 2 (Whole No. 239).

GOODNOW, JACQUELINE J., & POSTMAN, L. Probability learning in a problem solving situation. *J. exp. Psychol.*, 1955, **49**, 16–22.

GORMEZANO, I., & GRANT, D. A. Progressive ambiguity in the attainment of concepts on the Wisconsin Card Sorting Test. *J. exp. Psychol.*, 1958, **55**, 621–627.

GOSS, A. E., & MOYLAN, MARIE C. Conceptual block-sorting as a function of type and degree of mastery of discriminative verbal responses. *J. genet. Psychol.*, 1958, **93**, 191–198.

GRANT, D. A. Perceptual versus analytic responses to the number concept of a Weigl-type card sorting test. *J. exp. Psychol.*, 1951, **41**, 23–29.

GRANT, D. A., & BERG, E. A. A behavioral analysis of degree of reinforcement and ease of shifting to new responses in a Weigl-type card sorting problem. *J. exp. Psychol.*, 1948, **38**, 404–411.

GRANT, D. A., & COST, J. R. Continuities and discontinuities in conceptual behavior in a card sorting problem. *J. gen. Psychol.*, 1954, **50**, 237–244.

HALSTEAD, W. C. *Brain and intelligence.* Chicago: The University of Chicago Press, 1947.

HARLOW, H. F. The formation of learning sets. *Psychol. Rev.*, 1949, **56**, 51–65.

HARLOW, H. F. Learning set and error factor theory. In S. Koch (Ed.), *Psychology, A study of a science*. Vol. I. New York: McGraw-Hill, 1959.

HARROW, M., & FRIEDMAN, G. B. Comparing reversal and nonreversal shifts in concept formation with partial reinforcement controlled. *J. exp. Psychol.*, 1958, **55**, 592–598.

HAYGOOD, R. C., & BOURNE, L. E., JR. Forms of relevant stimulus redundancy in concept identification. *J. exp. Psychol.*, 1964, **67**, 392–397.

HAYGOOD, R. C., & BOURNE, L. E., JR. Attribute and rule learning aspects of conceptual behavior. *Psychol. Rev.*, 1965, **72**, 175–195.

HEIDBREDER, EDNA. An experimental study of thinking. *Arch. Psychol.*, 1924, **11**, No. 73.

HEIDBREDER, EDNA. Toward a dynamic psychology of cognition. *Psychol. Rev.*, 1945, **52**, 1–22.

HEIDBREDER, EDNA. The attainment of concepts: II. The problem. *J. gen. Psychol.*, 1946, **35**, 191–223.

HEIDBREDER, EDNA. The attainment of concepts: III. The process. *J. Psychol.*, 1947, **24**, 93–118.

HOCHBERG, J. E. Nativism and empiricism in perception. In L. Postman (Ed.), *Psychology in the making*. New York: Knopf, 1962.

HOVLAND, C. I. A "communication analysis" of concept learning. *Psychol. Rev.*, 1952, **59**, 461–472.

HOVLAND, C. I., & HUNT, E. B. Computer simulation of concept attainment. *Behavioral Sci.*, 1960, **5**, 265–267.

HOVLAND, C. I., & WEISS, W. Transmission of information concerning concepts through positive and negative instances. *J. exp. Psychol.*, 1953, **45**, 165–182.

HULL, C. L. Quantitative aspects of the evolution of concepts. *Psychol. Monogr.*, 1920, **28**, No. 1 (Whole No. 123).

HULL, C. L. Knowledge and purpose as habit mechanisms. *Psychol. Rev.*, 1930, **57**, 511–525.

HUNT, E. B. Memory effects in concept learning. *J. exp. Psychol.*, 1961, **62**, 598–604.

HUNT, E. B. *Concept learning: An information processing problem*. New York: Wiley, 1962.

HUNT, E. B., & HOVLAND, C. I. Order of consideration of different types of concepts. *J. exp. Psychol.*, 1960, **59**, 220–225.

HUTTENLOCHER, JANELLEN. Effects of manipulation of attributes on efficiency of concept formation. *Psychol. Rep.*, 1962, **10**, 503–509.

INGLIS, J. Psychological investigations of cognitive deficit in elderly psychiatric patients. *Psychol. Bull.*, 1958, **55**, 197–214.

INHELDER, BARBEL, & PIAGET, J. *The growth of logical thinking from childhood to adolescence*. New York: Basic Books, 1958.

ISAACS, I. D., & DUNCAN, C. P. Reversal and nonreversal shifts within and between dimensions in concept formation. *J. exp. Psychol.*, 1962, **64**, 580–585.

KENDLER, H. H., & D'AMATO, M. F. A comparison of reversal shifts and non-reversal shifts in human concept formation behavior. *J. exp. Psychol.*, 1955, **49**, 165–174.

KENDLER, H. H., GLUCKSBERG, S., & KESTON, R. Perception and mediation in concept learning. *J. exp. Psychol.*, 1961, **61**, 186–191.

KENDLER, H. H., & KARASIK, A. D. Concept formation as a function of competition between response-produced cues. *J. exp. Psychol.*, 1958, **55**, 278–283.

KENDLER, H. H., & KENDLER, TRACY S. Vertical and horizontal processes in problem solving. *Psychol. Rev.*, 1962, **69**, 1–16.

132

KENDLER, H. H., & VINEBERG, R. The acquisition of compound concepts as a function of previous training. *J. exp. Psychol.*, 1954, **48**, 252-258.

KENDLER, TRACY S. Learning development and thinking. In E. Harms (Ed.), Fundamentals of psychology: The psychology of thinking. *Ann. N. Y. Acad. Sci.*, 1960, **91**, 52-56.

KENDLER, TRACY S. Concept formation. *Annu. Rev. Psychol.*, 1961, **13**, 447-472.

KENDLER, TRACY S., & KENDLER, H. H. Reversal and nonreversal shifts in kindergarten children. *J. exp. Psychol.*, 1959, **58**, 56-60.

KING, W. A developmental study of rule learning. Ph.D. dissertation, University of Colorado, 1964.

KLEBANOFF, S. G., SINGER, J. L., & WILENSKY, H. Psychological consequences of brain lesions and ablations. *Psychol. Bull.*, 1954, **51**, 1-41.

KOOISTRA, W. H. Developmental trends in the attainment of conservation, transivity, and relativism in the thinking of children: A replication and extension of Piaget's ontogenetic formulations. *Psychol. dissertations in cognitive processes.* Wayne State University, 1964.

KRECHEVSKY, I. "Hypotheses" in rats. *Psychol. Rev.*, 1932, **38**, 516-532.

KURTZ, K. H., & HOVLAND, C. I. Concept learning with differing sequences of instances. *J. exp. Psychol.*, 1956, **51**, 239-243.

LEVINE, M. A model of hypothesis behavior in discrimination learning set. *Psychol. Rev.*, 1959, **66**, 353-366.

LEVINE, M. Mediating processes in humans at the outset of discrimination learning. *Psychol. Rev.*, 1963, **70**, 254-276.

LORDAHL, D. S. Concept identification using simultaneous auditory and visual signals. *J. exp. Psychol.*, 1961, **62**, 282-290.

LUDVIGSON, H. W., & CAUL, W. F. Relative effect of overlearning on reversal and non-reversal shifts with two and four sorting categories. *J. exp. Psychol.*, 1964, **68**, 301-306.

LURIA, A. R. The role of language in the formation of temporary connections. In B. Simon (Ed.), *Psychology in the Soviet Union.* Stanford: Stanford University Press, 1957. Pp. 115-129.

MAIER, N. R. F. Reasoning in humans: I. On direction. *J. comp. Psychol.*, 1930, **10**, 115-143.

MANDLER, G., COWAN, P. A., & GOLD, C. Concept learning and probability matching. *J. exp. Psychol.*, 1964, **67**, 514-522.

MAYZNER, M. S. Verbal concept attainment: A function of the number of positive and negative instances presented. *J. exp. Psychol.*, 1962, **63**, 314-319.

MEDNICK, S. A., & HALPERN, S. Ease of concept attainment as a function of associative rank. *J. exp. Psychol.*, 1962, **64**, 628-630.

MILNER, BRENDA. Intellectual function of the temporal lobes. *Psychol. Bull.*, 1954, **51**, 42-62.

MOON, L. E., & HARLOW, H. F. Analysis of oddity learning by rhesus monkeys. *J. comp. physiol. Psychol.*, 1955, **48**, 188-194.

MORRISETT, L., & HOVLAND, C. I. A comparison of three varieties of training in human problem solving. *J. exp. Psychol.*, 1959, **58**, 52-55.

NEISSER, U., & WEENE, P. Hierarchies in concept attainment. *J. exp. Psychol.*, 1962, **64**, 644-645.

NEWMAN, S. E. Effects of contiguity and similarity on the learning of concepts. *J. exp. Psychol.*, 1956, **52**, 349-353.

OSEAS, L., & UNDERWOOD, B. J. Studies of distributed practice: V. Learning and retention of concepts. *J. exp. Psychol.*, 1952, **43**, 143–148.

OSGOOD, C. E. *Method and theory in experimental psychology*. New York: Oxford, 1953.

OSLER, SONIA F., & FIVEL, M. W. Concept attainment: I. The role of age and intelligence in concept attainment by induction. *J. exp. Psychol.*, 1961, **62**, 1–8.

OSLER, SONIA F., & TRAUTMAN, GRACE E. Concept attainment: II. Effect of stimulus complexity upon concept attainment at two levels of intelligence. *J. exp. Psychol.*, 1961, **62**, 9–13.

OSLER, SONIA F., & WEISS, SANDRA R. Studies in concept attainment: III. Effects of instructions at two levels of intelligence. *J. exp. Psychol.*, 1962, **63**, 528–533.

PIAGET, J. *Logic and psychology*. New York: Basic Books, 1957.

PISHKIN, V. Effects of probability of misinformation and number of irrelevant dimensions upon concept identification. *J. exp. Psychol.*, 1960, **59**, 371–378.

RASMUSSEN, ELIZABETH A., & ARCHER, E. J. Concept identification as a function of language pretraining and task complexity. *J. exp. Psychol.*, 1961, **61**, 437–441.

REESE, H. W. Verbal mediation as a function of age level. *Psychol. Bull.*, 1962, **59**, 502–509.

RESTLE, F. A theory of discrimination learning. *Psychol. Rev.*, 1955, **62**, 11–19.

RESTLE, F. The selection of strategies in cue learning. *Psychol. Rev.*, 1962, **69**, 329–343.

RHINE, R. J. A concept-formation approach to attitude acquisition. *Psychol. Rev.*, 1958, **65**, 363–369.

RHINE, R. J., & SILUM, B. A. Acquisition and change of concept attitude as a function of consistency of reinforcement. *J. exp. Psychol.*, 1958, **55**, 524–529.

RICHARDSON, J., & BERGUM, B. O. Distributed practice and rote learning in concept formation. *J. exp. Psychol.*, 1954, **47**, 442–446.

ROMANOW, CONCETTA V. Anxiety level and ego involvement as factors in concept formation. *J. exp. Psychol.*, 1958, **56**, 166–173.

SCHULZ, R. W., MILLER, R. L., & RADTKE, R. C. The role of instance contiguity and dominance in concept attainment. *J. verb. Learn. verb. Behav.*, 1963, **1**, 432–435.

SHEPARD, R. N., HOVLAND, C. I., & JENKINS, H. N. Learning and memorization of classifications. *Psychol. Monogr.*, 1961, **75**, No. 13 (Whole No. 517).

SHERIF, M., & SHERIF, CAROLYN W. *An outline of social psychology* (Rev. Ed.). New York: Harper, 1956.

SHURE, G. H., & HALSTEAD, W. C. Cerebral localization of intellectual processes. *Psychol. Monogr.*, 1958, **72**, No. 12 (Whole No. 465).

SKINNER, B. F. *Verbal behavior*. New York: Appleton-Century-Crofts, 1957.

SMOKE, K. L. Negative instances in concept learning. *J. exp. Psychol.*, 1933, **16**, 583–588.

SPENCE, K. W. The nature of discrimination learning in animals. *Psychol. Rev.*, 1936, **43**, 427–449.

SPENCE, K. W. *Behavior theory and conditioning*. New Haven: Yale University Press, 1956.

TAYLOR, JANET A. A personality scale of manifest anxiety. *J. abnorm. soc. Psychol.*, 1953, **48**, 285–290.

THYSELL, R. V., & SCHULZ, R. W. Concept-utilization as a function of the strength of relevant and irrelevant associations. *J. verb. Learn. verb. Behav.*, 1964, **3**, 203–208.

UHL, C. N. Learning of interval concepts: I. Effects of differences in stimulus weights. *J. exp. Psychol.*, 1963, **66**, 264–273.

UNDERWOOD, B. J. An orientation for research on thinking. *Psychol. Rev.*, 1952, **59**, 209–220.

UNDERWOOD, B. J. Studies of distributed practice: XV. Verbal concept learning as a function of intralist interference. *J. exp. Psychol.*, 1957, **54**, 33–40.

UNDERWOOD, B. J. Stimulus selection in verbal learning. In C. N. Cofer and Barbara S. Musgrave (Eds.), *Verbal behavior and learning.* New York: McGraw-Hill, 1963.

UNDERWOOD, B. J., & RICHARDSON, J. Some verbal materials for the study of concept formation. *Psychol. Bull.*, 1956, **53**, 84–95. (a)

UNDERWOOD, B. J., & RICHARDSON, J. Verbal concept learning as a function of instructions and dominance level. *J. exp. Psychol.*, 1956, **51**, 229–238. (b)

VIGOTSKY, L. S. Thought in schizophrenia (Transl. by J. Kasanin). *Arch. Neurol. Psychiat.*, Chicago, 1934, **31**, 1063–1077.

WALKER, C. M., & BOURNE, L. E., JR. Concept identification as a function of amounts of relevant and irrelevant information. *Amer. J. Psychol.*, 1961, **74**, 410–417.

WALLACE, J. Concept dominance, type of feedback and intensity of feedback as related to concept attainment. *J. educ. Psychol.*, 1964, **55**, 159–166.

WELLS, H. Effects of transfer and problem structure in disjunctive concept formation. *J. exp. Psychol.*, 1963, **65**, 63–69.

WESLEY, ELIZABETH L. Perseverative behavior in a concept-formation task as a function of manifest anxiety and rigidity. *J. abnorm. soc. Psychol.*, 1953, **48**, 129–134.

Index